meth...

BY

ALBERT C. OUTLER

Dr. Outler vividly outlines the development of his hopes for Vatican II—the triumphs he cheered and the setbacks he lamented. Here are described all the important issues—religious liberty, the Church's relation to the Jews, the Church in the Modern world—as they appeared to an "outsider." By the end of the Council, Dr. Outler found himself talking in the first person plural about conciliar business and committed to the visionary ideals of the progressives.

Early in the Council, Dr. Outler asked, "What if Vatican II succeeds?" Now he knows that it did succeed: "In the aftermath of the Council, all Christians will have to take the Roman Catholic Church far more seriously into account than we have done in the past century or so. . . . The Council has given *us* a charter for change too."

server of the World Methodist Council to Vatican Council II, and is Vice-Chairman of the Commission on Ecumenical Affairs of the Methodist Church. He was given the 1966 "Methodist of the Year" Award. Among Dr. Outler's published works are *The Christian Tradition and the Unity We Seek* and *That The World May Believe.*

METHODIST OBSERVER
AT
VATICAN II

ALBERT C. OUTLER

METHODIST OBSERVER AT VATICAN II

NEWMAN PRESS

Westminster, Glen Rock, New York, Amsterdam, Toronto

ACKNOWLEDGMENTS

It is a pleasure to record here my gratitude to the following periodicals
for permission to reprint pieces that first appeared in their pages: *Motive,
The Oklahoma Courier, Christianity and Crisis, The Southwest Review,
The Methodist Story, All-Church Press.*

Library of Congress
Catalog Card Number: 67-15717

Designed by Russetta Madison

Published by Newman Press
Editorial Office: 304 W. 58th St., N.Y., N.Y. 10019
Business Office: Westminster, Md.

Manufactured in the
United States of America by
Colonial Press, Clinton, Mass.

CONTENTS

PREFACE

The Second Vatican Council has brought us many blessings but has also brought us a plethora of ponderous theological writing about Council reforms. One must take the good with the bad but I have found myself secretly yearning for the pre-aggiornamento lucidity, the witty and graceful prose of Ronald Knox. Now Albert Outler comes along to give us all this and post-Conciliar theology too. This Methodist theologian, a reincarnation of Knox, has a writing style that makes reading about the Council a literary and intellectual pleasure.

Outler has taught at Yale, Duke and Southern Methodist and has been associated for many years with the *Faith and Order* commission of the *World Council of Churches*. It is interesting to trace the development of his image of the Roman Catholic Church. When he went to Rome in 1962 as observer for the Methodists, his image of the Catholic Church was largely shaped by Trent and the Wars of Religion, by the *Syllabus of Errors* and papal condemnations of *Modernism*. This volume, comprising addresses and articles written by him during and after the Council, reveal the curious but cautious observer of an ecclesiastical pageant gradually becoming an engaged observer-participant with very definite opinions about Council developments. Those of us who came to know him during the Council looked forward to meeting him at the coffee-bar or at an evening reception in Rome where he would dilate enthusiastically on the morning's deliberations in St. Peter's.

A distinctive feature of Dr. Outler's manner of commenting on the Council is his psychological approach. Anyone who has read his *Psychotherapy and the Christian Message* would naturally expect to find him looking at the Council analytically, examining the interpersonal relationships of the bishops,

7

their particular circumstances and personal history, their relation to their own society and culture—all the psychodynamics involved in a bishop's vote on Religious Liberty or Collegiality or Ecumenism. He remarks, for instance, that in the ruckus over Religious Liberty at the end of the third session, "it was instructive to watch the onset of the liberals' panic-syndrome and the cynics' vindication-complex." This reaction of the liberals, he observes, "is somewhat similar to a manic-depression pattern with mood swings that range from soaring hopes of total victory to panic-fears of total defeat."

Yet this book is no psychoanalyst's notebook. Skilled systematic theologian that he is, Outler manages to read between the lines of the texts of Council documents and to convey a sense of the momentous excitement at the Council. He wears his profound knowledge of Church history modestly and, to borrow his own phrase, makes remembrance of things past illuminate the way ahead. The whole theological landscape lights up like a Roman candle under his magic talent for metaphor, his startling insights, his mischievous irreverence for sacred cows.

In the concluding section, "Charters for Change," he raises a frightfully important question that Catholics tend to dodge. Were the radical reforms that came out of Vatican II mere "developments"? He contends that Catholics would do well not to play coy with words in this quarter. He feels that they should face up to the fact that certain alterations from official teaching were actually mutations that should be called "changes." He sees therefore a need for the Church to provide an adequate theory of "change" that will validate the dynamics Vatican II has set in motion.

It is too early for a final accounting of the Council, according to Outler. He reminds Protestants, however, that something momentous is certainly stirring in the Roman Catholic Church and that they must not stand idly by as mere spectators of this stirring of the Spirit.

JOHN B. SHEERIN, C.S.P.

8

INTRODUCTION

FROM THE OBSERVERS' TRIBUNE

Already it is easy to forget how unlikely it all was—an ecumenical council of the Roman Catholic Church that no one expected, for which no one was prepared, which then proceeded to write a new chapter in church history. The idea of a council had come to Pope John XXIII as a sudden inspiration. His announcement of it had taken Rome and the rest of us by surprise. The interval between the announcement and the first session was busy and confused—an inspiration in search of an agenda! Reactions from the non-Roman Catholic world varied from yawns to yelps to suspicious murmurings. We were, of course, unable to ignore it even though we had no clear notion of what we had to hope or fear from it. The one thing that did not occur to us was that we might have a significant role in it ourselves.

I was, therefore, mildly startled by the news that a sizable corps of delegated-observers were to be invited to the council and taken even more aback when I was appointed as one of the Methodist observers by the Executive Committee of the World Methodist Council. If I had been really scrupulous, I should have declined the assignment, for I was really not properly qualified for it. But I was *curious* and I had pondered and puzzled over the monuments and documents of earlier councils in the history of the Church. This was a chance to observe and record a council *at firsthand*—and to be in Rome on a very rare occasion. Like most Protestants, my knowledge of Roman Catholic history began to fade out after the armistice of the 18th century. My acquaintance with modern Rome was perfunctory and not very favorable: Denzinger, Tanqueray and, of course, Canon George Smith's *Teachings of the Catholic Church*. I'd heard echoes of interesting new developments in liturgy and theology; such names as Beauduin, Rahner and Couturier were familiar—but chiefly from secondary sources. But the decisive symbols that shaped my stereotype of Rome were Trent and the Wars of Religion, the *Syllabus of Errors* and the condemnations of "modernism."

For a quarter century I had been active in "the ecumenical movement" and was rightly reckoned as a partisan in the cause of Christian unity. But no part of *this* cause had included Rome as an active partner. Indeed, there was its explicit rejection in the *Mortalium Animos* of Pius XI (1928)—further reinforced by the Holy Office monitum of 1948 (*Cum Compertum*). As for "the new theology," it had been condemned yet once more by the *Humani Generis* of 1950. And even the good Pope John—for all his open-heartedness—had tried to stop the clock with his *Veterum Sapientia* (1962) and had approved the Holy Office monitum against Teilhard de Chardin, just four months before the council was to convene. Up to this time, the only Roman Catholic theologian I had known personally was Father Gustave Weigel, S.J.—ecumenical pioneer extraordinary and an unsaintly saint! But his views of the ecumenical future were very long-range and his expectations of Vatican II were not especially sanguine. No matter. The Church of Rome in council was too interesting an event to miss and so I accepted my appointment with more interest than competence and without even a dim premonition that it was my ticket to a ringside seat at a turning point in church history.

Thereupon the unexpected began to happen almost regularly. For example, there was an invitation to dinner from Bishop Thomas K. Gorman (of Dallas-Fort Worth). This was the first time my wife and I had ever been in the home of a Roman Catholic prelate. Then there was the arrival of a bulky packet of official documents from Rome, from the Secretariat for Promoting Christian Unity, which turned out to be the first fascicles of the preparatory schemas for session one. They were marked *sub secretum* and I began to feel "involved." Once in Rome, the circle of my acquaintance began enlarging in every direction—with people and places that were scarcely more than names before, if that: bishops, archbishops, cardinals, popes, seminarians and journalists. There were even a few authentic "old Romans" (*Romani di Roma*) whom I got to know, who taught me the rudiments of the sign language that supplements the Vatican's official rhetoric.

It was a moving experience to discover that these open doors and arms meant more than an expression of courtesy and Christian hospitality. These people really wanted us to *observe* their council and they went to great lengths to make it possible for us to do so—including invitations to address *them* and so to enable us to observe *their reactions* to our observations. Pope John made sure that we had a privileged position in St. Peter's. Pope Paul welcomed our interest and participation:

> We urge you to persevere in your work as sincere and friendly observers, not to content yourselves with a passive presence but actively to understand and pray with us, so that you can communicate to your respective communities the best possible account of this council. This in

itself will be a contribution to the progressive drawing together of our minds in Christ our Lord.[1]

It was, of course, the Secretariat (first on the Via dei Corridori and then the Via dell'Erba) that was our "headquarters" in Rome—and it was its staff who provided every imaginable assistance in our work. They furnished the translators who sat with us mornings in our tribune and helped us understand not only what was said but also what was going on. They arranged weekly seminars (two hours each Tuesday afternoon) where we met key people from the conciliar commissions and debated the conciliar documents under consideration in the *aula*. During each session there were special tours for the observers and their wives—to the Sacro Convento at Assisi and other famous monasteries: San Nilo at Grottaferrata, Montecassino, Casamare, Subiaco, the Rieti Valley, etc. Then there were the annual formal receptions—one by them to us and one by us to them (the latter in the *aula* of the Waldensian Seminary on the Piazza Cavour!). It was the Secretariat which arranged our special audiences with the Pope—the first with Pope John in the gorgeous hall of the consistory; the second in Pope Paul's private library; the third in the Sistine Chapel; the fourth in the Benedictine Abbey of St. Paul's as a postlude to the now historic service of common worship in San Paolo fuori la Mura, at the close of the council. The only significant part of the business that was closed to us were the commission meetings—and even here, as the council wore on, we learned how to get reliable reports of their progress, and also how to convey *our* concerns to them. In all these ways and more, the observers constituted a presence in the council that was itself a dynamic factor in the process.

It was inevitable that we should bring with us a wide assortment of biases and reservations about the whole af-

---

[1] Observers' Audience, September 29, 1964.

fair. The Orthodox were excommunicated; the Protestants were anathematized. All of us had our reasons for being wary of one or another aspect of Roman teaching—faith and merit, papal absolutism, the Marian dogmas, Roman triumphalism, etc., etc. These were real difficulties and we did not suppose that they could be disposed of by polite conversation, however cordial. We wanted to see and to hear but we were determined not to be deceived or beguiled. One of the aims of the council, Pope John had said, was the recomposition of Christian unity. But on what terms? The Orthodox stiffened at the bare mention of the jurisdictional primacy of the Pope of Rome. We Protestants were fascinated and yet also disconcerted by the fuss and feathers of the baroque court ceremonials in St. Peter's and elsewhere. For example, before Pope Paul discarded the papal *flabella*, they never failed to remind me irreverently of Cleopatra (and Elizabeth Taylor!).

Even deeper went our doubts that Rome rightly understood the Gospel: God's utter sovereignty, the sheer gratuity of his mercy and pardon, the all-sufficiency of Christ's mediation and grace, the primacy of faith, the untrammeled authority of Holy Scripture, etc. Rome's reliance, we thought, was on the *opus operatum*—the human management of God's grace. Rome's piety, we thought, was a syndrome of merit and masochism—the gaining of God's favor by dint of human effort. What *could* come of such a Church in council? Some of us expected very little. None of us foresaw what actually happened.

In my own case, I had no clear preview of what was even possible, but I was deeply impressed by the self-conscious effort of a great Church attempting an experiment in self-examination and renewal. I knew, from history and experience, how hard it is for a large and tightly organized institution to recover its past vitalities—how much easier it is for institutions to redecorate and refurbish than to renew. But, from the beginning, I was convinced that Pope John's slogan, *aggiornamento,* was seriously meant and should be taken seriously. Whether the effort succeeded or failed, it would, in either case, be edifying to watch and record. One thing I noticed quickly was that the talk in Rome was full of historical allusions that seemed familiar to the Romans but often were unclear to me. *Everything* had a historical association and most things more than one. There was, therefore, no help for it but a crash program of forced and draft study and the eager brainpicking of all and sundry with questions of all sorts—about context, background, procedures, etc. Little by little, the business began to make more and more sense and I began to feel a little more secure in my perceptions and judgments. They were often enough wrong to remind me of my status as a novice but often enough right to encourage my persistent interest. Slowly but surely, this sense of expanding comprehension converted me first from an ecumenical tourist at a great ecclesiastical pageant into a participant observer in an epoch-making event, and then, into a partner in the ongoing ecumenical enterprise which has been generated by that event.

Happily, the stretching of my mind ran roughly parallel with the vicissitudes of the conciliar process. At first, my fears that Vatican II would be only another solemn assembly (like the Roman Synod of 1960) dampened my hopes that it might amount to something more significant. For example, it was several days after the opening session before I understood the magnitude of the crisis of those very first fifteen minutes, when the council gained a character of its own by the abrupt rejection of the fixed agenda proposed by the management and the subsequent election of a new slate of members for the conciliar commissions. Even in the early days, it was easy to sense the tensions and bafflements in St. Peter's as the bishops were groping their way along, but I could rarely calculate their direc-

tion or probable development. It was only after the first
session had been adjourned a month or so that I began to
realize how critical was the impasse to which the council
had come. Indeed, it was not until I had read and pondered Pope John's final great "testament" (*Pacem in
Terris*, April 11, 1963) that I finally understood what he
had really meant for *his* council to be. All the more, therefore, I mourned *our* loss in his death.

Thus, our initial fears—and hopes—were reactivated
when we returned to Rome for session two. What would
the new Pope do to forward and yet also to modify the
initiatives of his predecessor? Already I had had an uneasy feeling that the charisms of Pope John would require
other ways and means of getting themselves translated
into actual conciliar decisions. It seemed plain to me that
the immobilists still held the Vatican passes! Thus, I was
all eyes and ears for Paul VI's first allocution (September
29, 1963). That occasion—what he said and how he said
it—convinced me that he would carry the council through
to a good end. I was convinced that he wanted reform but
a reform of a quite special sort (what I later labeled "Reformation Roman-Style") *and* that he could bring along
with him the as yet uncommitted majority of the bishops!
From the first, he gave me the impression that he meant to
move the Roman Church forward as far and as fast as possible, without risking schism in its soul. I was, therefore,
prepared to "defend" him against the dispraise of his own
more impatient "reformers," who were scandalized by his
tender care for the consciences of the diehard minority.
These overeager souls, as it seemed to me, were measur-
ing Paul's *performance* by John's *dreams*—or their own!
What kept going through my mind were my freshly
learned lessons of the history of the papacy in the 19th
century (which had lasted until 1958!). I also kept re-
membering those baroque characters in the curia who
still manned the battlements of a Church they wanted to

preserve intact. Against *this* background—and with his own curialist upbringing—it seemed to me that Paul VI was doing a remarkable job—and it seems so still.

Through such experiences and such musings, I came to be more and more immersed in the council—its daily worship and work, its discussions and decisions, its drama and its cast of characters. There were those who found the protracted debates repetitious and boring. To me, they were the mirror in which one could trace the subtle cumulative shifts in "the minds" of a council in the process of being formed. Their results were later registered in the successive revisions of the schemas. Moreover, I was mightily impressed by the sights and sounds of 2,000 bishops engaged in what still seems an extraordinary exercise in *reeducation*. This, surely, must be reckoned as one of the council's most signal achievements. One way and another, I got so engrossed that I began to forget to remember that I was an "outsider." I began to weigh the stakes in the crucial ballots as they came along and even to swap predictions with my *periti* friends. Every now and then, I'd lapse from "they" and "their" to "we" and "our."

The original purpose of the observers at the council was to provide their respective church constituencies with reports of the conciliar deliberations. In the first session, the *sub secretum* rule was at least nominally enforced, and one might mention that it was respected by the observers somewhat more scrupulously than by some of the bishops. From the second session on, however, the definition of secrecy was considerably relaxed and we began to be asked for public comment on various occasions. Our hosts in the Secretariat encouraged us to speak as candidly as we wished within the obvious limits of prudence. Thus began the business of which this book is a by-product: reports and articles, addresses and lectures, etc., etc. In three years these *dicta et scripta* accumulated into a bulging file of instant history which stands on my shelf alongside a dozen large notebooks of daily minutes, diaries and a complete file of "the Bishops' Digest!" It is from this large and uneven mass that this present collection has been culled.

The principles of selection here are twofold: historical and ecumenical. Since it is now clear to all that Vatican II will stand as a major landmark in the history of our time, it may be interesting to others to rehearse its progress through the widening eyes of an engaged but critical observer. The items here are all snapshots. Each is dated, placed and strictly occasional. They have been arranged in chronological order and each reflects its specific audience—from churchfolk who read parish and diocesan papers to scholars who attend the annual meetings of the American Historical Association. Each was done in haste and on demand. None has been improved by hindsight despite the obvious temptations to do just that. The reader will find more repetition here than he would expect in a connected history, but this, too, reflects the way in which the basic interpretive themes (and favorite phrases!) grew in my mind. Much has been omitted: official reports, addresses at various services of "ecumenical witness," technical articles, cozy pieces to go with my hundreds of color slides and miles of tape recordings. What is here is a representative sampling of eyewitness reaction and, as such, is offered as a modest contribution to the council's history.

It is also now clear that Vatican II began a new chapter in the history of the modern ecumenical movement—but that it left many blank pages still to be filled in. I was especially interested in everything that was said and done, inside the council and outside, that had any bearing at all on the furtherance or hindrance of the cause of Christian unity. This constant concern is reflected in almost everything I said or wrote. Thus, the pieces here will serve as a reflection of one man's awareness of what happened in Vatican II that pertains directly or indirectly to the ecumenical enterprise and its future. This emphasis is important because, as the council slips further back into our memories, we shall need to recall its successive crises over the questions of ecumenism in order to understand the unfolding problems of the dialogue as it goes forward. Here, too, the remembrance of things past may illuminate the way ahead.

It has come to be a commonplace—and that in itself is a sign of progress!—that there are three successive stages in the normal progress of ecumenical experience: initiation, cooperation, negotiation. For divided and estranged Christians, there must come, first of all, the joyous discovery that our "separated *brethren*" are *Christian* brethren, too—the mutual recognition of a common loyalty to Christ, the acknowledgment that we already have an earnest of God's gift of unity in the Holy Spirit. It is this dawning truth that begins to purge our ancient enmities and to forge new bonds of faith, hope and love between us. This is our ecumenical *initiation*—the first and crucial step away from our old divisions and estrangement. In it we are, naturally enough, self-conscious, nervous— and exhilarated!

But such experiences are not ends in themselves and must never be allowed to remain so. They must progress toward meaningful action or else they will turn sentimental and begin the slide toward indifferentism—the exact antithesis of *authentic* ecumenism. Christian brethren who have found and affirmed each other must move on to common modes of Christian witness and service in and for the world for which Christ died. This was plainly the vision of Pope John. He was willing almost recklessly to commit the Catholic Church to new ventures of love toward *all* men of goodwill. This is what so deeply stirred the world, and this is why that world continues to measure the council by the Johannine vision. It was one of the distinctive achievements of Vatican II that it opened a new frontier of practical ecumenical cooperation which has continued to expand in almost every direction ever since the close of the council.

But successful experiments in initiation and cooperation lead sooner or later to the core issue of ecumenism: full and real communion (*communicatio in sacris*). At this point, however, the anginal frustrations of our ecumenical hopes begin to press upon us. Christians who can pray and work together come finally to realize that they *ought* to be united in sacramental fellowship, not for themselves but for the sake of the Church's mission— "that the world may believe" (John 17:21).

It is important to remember that before Vatican II, there had been no expectation of even the first step of real ecumenical initiation between Roman Catholics and other Christians. *A fortiori*, the prospects for effective cooperation were even less hopeful, and the notion of serious *negotiation* about full communion with Rome had been literally unthinkable—save for those individual conversions that *we* labeled "lapses." The burdens of our separate histories and alien commitments were far too heavy to be shed lightly or quickly. "Reunion by return" (to Rome, Constantinople or wherever) has never been a live option in modern ecumenism. The only way to the fullness of Christian comm*unity* is forward—to some point of convergence toward which we are now being led by the still secret Providence of God.

It was, therefore, an unprecedented achievement of Vatican II that, in a single short quadrennium, the tendencies of four centuries have been decisively reversed— and the first two stages of ecumenical initiation and cooperation almost suddenly telescoped. What had seemed unlikely has actually happened, without betrayal on either side. And this also means that what had been unthinkable (negotiation) has begun to be at least conceivable. This is the point to hold to—for if one miracle has been vouchsafed to us, are we credulous if we hope and work and pray for yet another?

In the meantime, and as the consequences of the council unfold, we must reckon as realistically as possible with the challenges and chances of the new situation. Within the Catholic Church itself, the council has launched an immense ferment of renovation and development—in liturgy and the life of prayer, in preaching and evangelism, in the mission of the lay apostolate, in institutional organization and ecumenical outreach. It has also triggered a crisis of authority and freedom, raised the problem of continuity and change up to the level of a critical issue, and has exposed the Catholic community to the winds of change and the acids of modernity.

It has done more. For the time being at least, it has passed the initiative in the ecumenical movement over to the Roman Catholic Church and has posed a whole cluster of unexpected challenges to other Christian communions and to the World Council of Churches—raising all over again, now in a new context, the question of their relations with Rome and the grounds on which they can be justified or altered. No one can now foresee clearly what these reconsiderations will amount to. Certainly in Pope John's mind one of the prime *desiderata* of the council was some measure of reconciliation between Rome and the Orthodox Churches. This goal was reaffirmed by Pope Paul and dramatized to the world in his pilgrimage to Palestine (and his meeting there with the Ecumenical Patriarch). It even came to a sort of partial fulfillment in the mutual cancellations of the excommunications of 1054. It would have to be said, however, that the general tenor of Orthodox reaction thus far has been cordial, correct—and intransigent. This is psychologically understandable but nonetheless dangerous, because it discourages the progressives in both camps and has already given the Roman *immobilisti* a handy excuse for *their* continued intransigence. In any case, progress in Catholic-Orthodox relations, or the lack of it, has now become one of the most significant "pointer-readings" in current ecumenical calculations.

As for the Protestants, none of them came to Rome with any intention of even raising the question of the terms of reunion. For many of them the only terms *they* would have considered would have been *Rome*'s return to "pure doctrine"—the Augsburg Confession or Heidelberg or Westminster! The odd thing to me, in the course of the council, was that I saw more signs of a disposition toward doctrinal development among the Romans than among the Protestants. As Rome abandons its triumphalism, its negative image in Protestantism looms up as considerably larger than some of us had supposed it was. Thus, when a Lutheran professor (Carl Braaten in *Una Sancta,* Pentecost, 1966) proposed that Protestants rethink the terms on which they could look forward toward reunion with Rome (not *"return"*), a leading "ecumenical weekly" (*The Christian Century*) blasted the notion in an editorial captioned "Protestant Hara-kiri"!

Meanwhile, however, the new spirit of Vatican II spreads further and wider and continues to multiply new experiences of Christian fellowship for countless individuals and congregations around the world. It begins to look as if the ecumenical movement has, so to say, "gotten out of hand"—out of the hands, that is, of the professional ecumenists into the hands and hearts of the Christian people at the parish and neighborhood levels. And the feedback from their discoveries will raise the pressure on their leaders to find ways to translate these burgeoning hopes into reality. In the new climate that is spreading throughout the Christian world, new forms of Christian cooperation are being sought and found—as one can see in the common areas of Christian social concern in the *Pastoral Constitution on the Church in the Modern World* and in the recent World Council of Churches Conference on Church and Society. It would be unwise and ineffectual to press too hard too soon for too much by way of *communicatio in sacris,* but the vision of this possibility has emerged and its challenge can no longer be ignored or dismissed.

There never was a straight and easy way to Christian unity—no expectations of it should ever have been stirred. As Pope Paul said to us in his farewell message:

> We would have loved—with Pope John XXIII to whom belongs the credit for the fact that our conversation is once more trustful and brotherly—to have celebrated with you a decisive and climactic reunion, or at least with some of you. But we have come to realize that this is an all too human impatience; that there is still a long journey toward the goal of full and valid communion—many more prayers to the Father of Lights, many more vigils to keep. Even so, there is at least one victory to record here at the close of the council: we have begun to love each other once more! May the Lord grant us that the world may recognize us as *his* disciples, insofar as we have restored this spirit of mutual love between us.

This was, indeed, the victory of Vatican II—a healing love which has begun to overcome estrangement and to lead us on toward the further stages on our providential journey. That journey has not yet been fully mapped but we are finally on the way together and the memory of how we have thus far been led should fortify our courage to continue. This little book of "testimonials" is offered as an aid to such memories and, therefore, to good hope as well.

CHAPTER 1

THE PROSPECTS OF THE COUNCIL

September 24, 1962

In September of 1962, Mr. Robert G. Hoyt of *The National Catholic Reporter* of Kansas City (representing the Catholic Features Cooperative), circularized the American delegated-observers asking for "their views of the council, their hopes for its success and their understanding of their own roles, etc., etc." in "statements of from 500 to 1000 words."

This was my first occasion to react publicly to "the challenge of Vatican II," and my first contribution to a Catholic publication. The covering letter that accompanied the "statement" is also reprinted—a somewhat more candid and significant forecast of the crises of the first session than the formal statement. Together they reflect the liveliest hopes I could muster on the eve of the council.

Dear Mr. Hoyt:

Thanks for your invitation to comment on the forthcoming *Vaticanum Secundum*. It is a privilege for me to respond—and I send you herewith a statement that comes as near as I've been able to summarize my views here on the eve of the council.

As a Protestant theologian—interested in but not fully conversant with *current* Roman Catholic theology in America and Europe—it seems wise to focus on the issues of theological "liberalism" and "reaction," since this is clearly the critical area where the basic decisions will come.

I have just read, with great care—and, frankly, no little alarm—the preparatory reports of the central commission, proposing, for example, that the sources of revelation (Scripture and Tradition) be redefined in conventionally "Tridentine" terms, despite the contrary views of Trent held by some of your best scholars in this field (Geiselmann, Congar, Tavard). Then there is the related proposal that the anti-modernist oath of 1910 (*Sacrorum Antistitum*) be written into the conciliar profession of faith. You, and all liberal Catholics, must know that these proposals, if adopted, will be wholly disastrous for the Catholic-Protestant dialogue almost before it is well begun—because it will throw both sides back on defensive positions that ceased to be fruitful somewhere in the 17th century, if not before. It would be a flagrant impertinence for us observers to interfere in the council's decisions in these matters. But it is important that everyone realize what is involved in this crisis of ecumenical conscience. Few of us expect, or even want, the road to Christian unity made easy, but many of us would feel desolated if it were summarily blocked.

It goes without saying that I hope and believe that this will not happen—though not all my confrères hereabouts are as sanguine as I. But we all know enough about the conciliar process to know that a reactionary move, made early by powerfully placed forces, is very hard to deflect or even modify in subsequent debate. If, therefore, this council is going to respond to Pope John's call for an *incrementum fidei* in such a way that those of us who have come to regard ourselves as "evangelical catholics" can participate in good heart and conscience, it will require a real *actus tradendi* of the Holy Spirit. And if this happens, that will be the day for the *Te Deum!*

Here's hoping, therefore, that our common hopes and high expectations for Vatican II will be at least *partially* realized. In any case, this is an exciting time and it is a great privilege for me to be involved in the council as a fascinated eyewitness.

Gratia tibi et pax!

Vaticanum Secundum is an event of incalculable importance in the history of modern Christianity. It is incalculable because no one can be quite sure what will come of it. It is important because, no matter what does happen, the ecumenical situation is bound to be altered significantly thereafter—for better or for worse. Most Protestants understand by now that, formally speaking, this council is a family affair within the Roman Catholic Church. That means that its effects on the relations between Rome and the rest of the Christian community will be largely indirect. But no one rightly doubts that they will be deep-going and far-reaching. They might, quite possibly, be epoch-making.

The invitation to non-Roman Christians to be present at the council as official observers is a very gracious and hospitable gesture toward the "separated brethren," but it is also much more than this. It affords us an unprecedented opportunity to get acquainted with the Church of Rome on its own ground and, so to say, with its best foot forward. Yet also, and equally important, it should help us to prepare for a responsible role in the ensuing chapter of Christian history about to be written. It means that we will be interested witnesses of a great visualization of Roman catholicity in action, participant observers in a conciliar process mostly unlike anything we ourselves have ever known. We shall naturally be fascinated spectators of the pomp and panoply of 2,000 bishops in solemn conclave in St. Peter's. At a deeper level, however, we shall also be attentive listeners trying to hear—really to hear—what the Holy Spirit will be saying to the Churches in and through this whole affair. At the same time, however, we shall also be deeply concerned with the council's results and what they will mean for the cause of Christian unity in our time. Pope John has vividly defined his threefold goal for the council in his first encyclical on the subject (*Ad Petri Cathedram*): the updating and renewal of the Church in its ecclesiological self-understanding and in its ecclesiastical polity. But what if the forces of theological *reaction* prevail, as quite conceivably they may?

We know, for example, that in recent decades a lively and fruitful discussion has been developing between Catholic and Protestant theologians, on terms which have allowed for real integrity on both sides and which have led to the discovery of much common ground—biblical, historical, practical. The triumph in the council of a rigid, reactionary "triumphalism" would stultify this whole process and would reopen the crisis of the Christian conscience once symbolized by Augsburg and Trent. What then would be the fate of the modern Catholic intellectuals—and the Protestant ecumenists—within their own communions and in the ecumenical movement as a whole? If it be objected that such queries presuppose the possibility that the Church of Rome could err, then *that* objection would serve to define our dilemma—and the ecumenical problem—as sharply as one might wish or fear.

We shall not, therefore, go to Rome as mere spectators, nor yet as suppliants. Our sympathies lie naturally with the progressives but we shall not be there as partisans, with champions to cheer and villains to hiss. Rather, we shall go as pilgrims, fellow-petitioners for *authentic* Christian community, in constant and earnest prayer (in the spirit and intention of the late Abbé Couturier) that God may use all that is done to open the way toward *genuine* Christian unity, as *Christ wills* it and as *he* will provide it for his now divided disciples—in terms which may or may not be identical with any of the formulas which any group of Christians can yet write for us all.

CHAPTER 2

ALUMNI ASSOCIATION ADDRESS

February 6, 1963

Session one was a baffling business for an observer still bewildered by the strange turn of events in the council—first in its opening minutes and then in the ensuing debates on the liturgy and on the sources of revelation. Moreover, the etiquette of being an observer was still interpreted to mean that the *sub secretum* applied to our discussion of the documents and debates. Consequently, I wrote nothing for publication and declined all speaking engagements during the session itself. Afterward (in February, 1963), I was invited to speak to our annual Alumni Association luncheon and asked to interpret the course of the council for them. As usual in alumni-luncheon speeches, this one had a good deal of strictly local comment, but toward the end I tried to summarize my estimate of the council in its first installment.

My hearers were, for the most part, younger ministers, vitally interested in the portents of renewal and reform that they had heard about from Rome. But they knew next to nothing about the prehistory of the council, or the background of the struggles constantly stressed in the papers—between "progressives" and "integralists," etc. What little I knew had also been lately learned—for this was not part of the standard historical curriculum in my education or theirs, up to that time. Things have begun to change in Protestant seminaries since then. What follows are the "conclusions" that I tried to draw about the council after a capsuled prehistory of it that has been omitted.

. . . This prehistory will help you understand the now familiar comment that when the Cardinal Patriarch of Venice, Angelo Roncalli, was elected Pope on October 28, 1958, he found himself in command of a beleaguered fortress—a Church on the defensive and allergic to change. But Pope John XXIII was not a veteran of the Roman curia and in his long career in church diplomacy (in the Balkans and postwar France) he was fully aware of the radical changes in the world that challenged the Church to change. Moreover, he was amazingly confident that the Church could afford to risk itself in new ventures of reform to meet these new challenges and opportunities. This was back of his famous gesture of opening the window of his study and saying, "Fresh air—that is what I want here and that is why I want a *council*."

It is worth noting that the curia did not oppose Pope John in his project for a council. They obviously did not want one and, in their control of the executive powers of an infallible papacy, they could see no need for one. But they were consistent enough in their devotion to their own doctrine of infallibility so that if the Pope wanted a council, he should have one. The main thing was to keep it safe.

To this end they did what came naturally: they took advantage of the fact that they were firmly in control of both the engine and the caboose of the ecclesiastical freight train. The "Roman" cardinals (Ottaviani, Cicognani, Antoniutti, Confalonieri *et al.*) and their understudies (Parente, Felici, Staffa)—all very Italian, very conservative, very powerful—simply took over the business of preparing for a council that would achieve a drastic housecleaning without disarranging the furniture, that would update the organization but leave the Tridentine posture of the Church unaltered. Such a council could have been adjourned by last Christmas—and was meant to be.

That is why the most important thing about this first session is that it managed to turn itself from a routine process of reviewing and approving proposals made by the management into a real council, in which most of the really crucial issues have now been opened wide to ventilation and debate—with a long road ahead before they will be settled by consensus.

Consider the enormous initial advantage, in a tightly organized connectional Church (like ours, only bigger), of an entrenched, efficient, dedicated bureaucracy in direction and control of a council of 2,000 bishops (or, for that matter, our General Conference of 900). They gave what they thought would be token representation to leaders of the progressive movement—Cardinals Alfrink (Utrecht), Doepfner (Munich), Koenig (Vienna), Léger (Montreal)—but they made very sure that they had a minority role to play in the preparatory commission which produced the schemas to be considered by the bishops.

These schemas gave scant promise of any significant change from the tone and temper of Vatican I. When I first read the schema *On the Sources of Revelation* my heart sank and my blood ran cold. Here was something, in the year 1962, that was no better than Trent, from the standpoint of any conceivable rapprochement with the Protestants. If this schema had been approved, the slow but gratifying progress of the past 25 years in the mutual discovery of common spiritual and theological ground between Protestants and Romans in many different parts of the world would simply have gone down the drain.

The very basis for an adequate doctrine of Scripture and Tradition—on ecumenical grounds—would have been undercut.

What the council has proved, however, is that Rome is not a monolithic, conformist community. Men with convictions as strong and as deep as those of these arch-conservatives—and yet as devout and loyal Catholics as any —believe that truth and love allow for a deposit of absolute truth in the scriptural revelation *and* a relativized development of truth in the history of Christian doctrine. These men believe that the Roman Church can fulfill its mission in the world far more effectively if the balance between papacy and episcopacy is restored, if the liturgy is returned to the people in the vernacular, if the ecumenical dialogue is opened up still wider. They are not "soft" on Protestants and other heretics, but they represent a spirit of inquiry once regnant in the Catholic Church but overwhelmed for the last six centuries by the tradition of *semper idem* (the motto on Ottaviani's coat-of-arms!). In Rome they speak of the *partita di verita* (those who put truth first and claim they have it, whole and entire) and the *partita di carita* (those who put love at the head of all the Christian virtues—and extend it to their "separated brethren"). Pope John, who knows Ephesians 4:15 at least as well as any other man, stands between the *partiti* and exhorts them both to seek and to speak *the truth in love*—and thus grow up into Christ!

The point I want to make is that this first session was not merely an immense and spectacular pageant or even a tremendous practical project in reorganization and updating. It was, and still is, a *crisis*—in the sense that all subsequent history is going to be decisively different, whichever way the outcome falls. If Cardinal Bea and his cause predominate, the ecumenical movement will gain exciting new dimensions and momentum. If the *semper idem* group prevails, then a multitude of Christians will be condemned to a regression, back into their denominational ghettoes.

This is why Pope John's leadership is so crucial, why he is rightly regarded as one of the most remarkable of the modern popes. He is intensely devout and unbelievably uncomplicated. He is astute and enormously capable. This is *his* council and up to this point he is quite literally indispensable to it. He opened its sessions by commissioning the bishops to dedicated labor and ordaining them to free and responsible debate. And the one clear fact about the whole affair thus far is that it has been a free and responsible council in the truest sense of these terms. In this respect it equals or exceeds any other deliberative church body I have myself seen in action, from our annual conferences to the assemblies of the World Council of Churches.

Its climactic turning point came in the week of November 14, in the course of the debate on the sources of revelation. It was an open, drawn contest between the *partita di verita* and the *partita di carita,* which was finally forced to a showdown by the general secretary (Archbishop Felici) who abruptly called for a vote on November 20. When counted, the ballot (1,368 for outright rejection of the original schema to 822 in its favor) proved a dogfall. The *carita* crowd didn't have enough votes to reject Ottaviani's text outright, but the *verita* boys were put on notice that no such schema would ever be approved by *this* council. The next day, Pope John directed that the schema be withdrawn and he then reconstituted the group that will rework it and submit a new text to the second session. This *new* group includes members of the Secretariat for Promoting Christian Unity! Even while we are meeting here they are meeting in Rome—stretching their nerves and hearts and minds—some of them very much aware, incidentally, of what Faith and Order has been doing over the past decade in this problem area of Scripture and Tradition.

There will now be a lull in the general news of the council until sometime in midsummer, I should say—unless the Pope's health (or ill-health, I'm afraid) intervenes and changes things. To this one can say in devout prayer: God forbid! Meanwhile, in another part of the ecumenical scene, the interval will be filled by another major ecumenical event: the forthcoming Fourth World Conference of Faith and Order to be held at Montreal in July.

There is a good deal for us all to do in keeping up with the interim developments. On April 1-3, Cardinal Bea will be in this country, first in Cambridge and then New York, making major pronouncements on the tasks and prospects of the Council. Then in September, the bishops are scheduled to go back to work with the following main issues "up for action":

1. Final debate and voting on the *Constitution on the Sacred Liturgy.*

2. A renewal of the debate on the Church's custody of the *depositum fidei*—which is to say the source of revelation and the Church's access to it. This is the crux of the ecumenical problem.

3. The collegiality of the episcopacy—a burning issue for the immobilists.

4. The Roman Catholic Church's understanding of the nature of the Church and its self-understanding as Church.

5. The apostolate of the laity and their role in the household of faith.

6. I for one will be watching with peculiar interest what they do with the three drafts prepared by Cardinal Ciriaci's commission on *The States of Perfection,* for this will have a direct bearing upon the whole question of monastic reform in the Roman Catholic Church and the

33

relevance of the universal call to holiness for all Christians.[1]

What sets this council off from every other one before it is its primary stress upon the pastoral, positive, initiatory opportunities and responsibility of the Church in the modern world. Thus far, at least, it has been far less interested in condemnations, inquisitions and denunciations than in girding itself for tomorrow and preparing itself for its future missions in a world shaken by seismic uncertainties and threatened by hideous dangers.

This council has not succeeded yet—and it may quite possibly fail, tragically, to measure up to its *kairos* and possibility. No veteran of the ecumenical wars is easily carried away by an uprush of optimism. I would be the last to suppose that this council, or even its successor, will be able to draft a proposal for Christian unity that can forthwith be acted upon by the widely divided segments of the People of God. What matters more is that the future should be opened up and lines of development laid out in some fashion not obviously self-defeating or patently superficial.

I have no notion of seeing anything resembling a fully authentic Christian community—one that allows for full and real *communicatio in sacris*—in my lifetime. It is even possible that the Christian people will continue in their estrangements and driftings until we are reduced again to a remnant in the world before we will accept our God-given unity in Christ. But for now, and for ourselves, one can hardly think of a single project in the Christian cause more urgent and germane than this search for valid and evangelical unity that will support and enhance the mission of the Church.

In this concern—the most distinctive development in contemporary church history—Vatican II already deserves a chapter to itself.

[1] These finally found their place, in a much amended form, in chapters five and six of the *Constitution on the Church*.

CHAPTER 3

THE SEPARATED BRETHREN
OF ST. LONGINUS

November 8, 1963

One of the highlights of each session was the reception given by the Paulist Fathers and their congregation of Santa Susanna, "the American Catholic Church" in Rome. The scene was the ballroom of the nearby Grand Hotel and the invitations went to the American bishops and *periti,* to the American Embassy, religious sisters, the council auditors, observers and "friends." There was, of course, the inevitable speech on the program and someone had the bright idea that this should be given by an observer—a mildly startling notion at first which then became a cherished "tradition" by the time of session four. Dean Douglas Horton (Congregationalist) was invited to do the honors at the first reception (December 6, 1962) and I at the second (November 8, 1963).

For all the talking I'd been doing *about* Roman Catholics and their council, this was the first time that I had ever spoken *to* a Roman Catholic audience—and a most extraordinary one at that, what with two cardinals, several archbishops and bishops in what seemed to me a formidable profusion!

At the time, the council was deep in crisis. On October 29, the closest vote of all four sessions (1,114 to 1,074) had decided that the Marian schema should be incorporated into the

Constitution on the Church. On October 30, the famous straw vote on collegiality had upset the *immobilisti* and their intransigent reaction had, in turn, aroused the progressives. The debate on "The Bishops and the Government of Dioceses" had just begun (November 5)—an explosive issue because it rubbed the sore nerve of the relations between diocesan autonomy and curial control. Indeed, the explosion had come on the very morning of the reception, when Cardinal Frings had calmly denounced the Holy Office "whose methods and manners do not conform at all to the modern era and are a cause of scandal to the world" and Cardinal Ottaviani had retorted in outrage by accusing Frings first of ignorance or worse—and then of *lèse-majesté:* "In attacking the Holy Office, one attacks the Pope, because he is its prefect."

I knew a lot more about these outward facts than I could understand of the total drama. But one thing was obvious enough even to an observer: my audience was tense with suppressed excitement and curiosity as to what was going on in the council—and what would happen next. That they listened attentively and responded most cordially was another sample of their poise and unfailing charity.

Your Excellencies, Venerable Fathers, Beloved Brethren in Christ: I speak to you this afternoon as a member of a new and not yet authorized order which has sprung up in the course of this council. It is the Separated Brotherhood of St. Longinus—for, as you know, the tribune of the observers is placed directly under Bernini's great statue. And, as you can guess, the centurion's spear was quivering this morning!

My obvious first word in response to your gracious hospitality is one of heartfelt appreciation for the memorable experiences you have afforded us as observers and guests of this council. It is not merely that we are being treated with uncommon courtesy on every hand, or that we are being given exceptional opportunities to see and hear what is going on, or that we have the tutelage and aid of an extremely competent and friendly staff in the

Secretariat—so that more than one of you has wondered aloud as to your advantage in being mere *patres conciliares!* Far deeper than these outward signs of Christian fellowship—grateful as we are for them—are the actions and impulses of the Holy Spirit within our hearts and yours, where he has begun to break down the old, encrusted barriers of ignorance, prejudice and enmity that have so long divided us and has awakened a new disposition toward mutual recognition and of genuine interest in dialogue in us all. The result is a literally unprecedented experience of Christian comradeship. It is no light thing for us that we are enabled to join with you daily in the mass and the angelus, to follow your debates with ears cocked for their ecumenical import, to be jostled in the disorderly cameraderie of Bar-jonah and Bar-abbas, to get to know you personally as men of grace and wisdom—and of rare good humor, too!

Some of us, acquainted with the conciliar processes in our own *ecclesiae vel communitates* (as the text of the *Decree on Ecumenism* has it) are much impressed by your ways of working in the council: the relentless pressure you keep on what is obviously an unwieldy body of prelates, the normally high level of the interventions, the refreshing candor and freedom of thought and expression (both in and out of the *aula*), the curious blending of pomp and circumstance, on the one hand, and on the other, these occasional flashes of improvisation which we can see struck off up at our end of the *aula*.[1] Others of us —veterans of the excitements and frustrations of the commissions and assemblies of the World Council of Churches, etc.—find strikingly similar parallels between your sessions and some of ours. There is a similar kaleido-

[1] The desks of the general secretariat were directly below our tribune and the daises of the presidents and moderators only a few feet away. It was easy, therefore, for us to notice the flurries of consultation and decision before the public announcements.

METHODIST OBSERVER AT VATICAN II

scope of views on every major topic; there are similar problems of coordinating the schedules of your commissions and the general congregations. There is the same boredom of endless discussion and also the perils of premature decisions; the same impatience that calls for a showdown before the mind of the council is fully manifested or even formed and, over against this, the dogged patience that endures all this talk in the vain hope that at the end of it all the *status quo erat ante concilium* will still have been miraculously preserved.

What has impressed us even more, I think, is your willingness to *be* observed: to expose yourselves to the inquiring eyes of friendly but not at all uncritical observers; your willingness to engage in the baffling enterprise of self-understanding, self-explanation, self-inspection; your willingness to risk the fearful hazards of what Pope John called *aggiornamento*. In our recent audience with Pope Paul VI, he was wonderfully open and explicit about this:

> Our intention is to hide nothing from you, nor to conceal any of the difficulties in the way of a complete and definitive understanding. We do not fear the tension of discussion nor the pain of waiting. Good faith and charity is the basis of the relation we propose with you; the esteem we hold for you as persons and for the institutions and Christian values you represent makes it easy for us to take up with you the great dialogue, the duration of which no one can today determine because of the doctrinal divergences which have not yet been resolved.

We are all very much aware of what this council has already effected in the Christian community and in the world, just by the sheer impact of its happening, under the providence and the presidence of the Holy Spirit. In the span of five short years, a wholly unprecedented change of climate in the Christian world has taken place.

All of you can testify to this—and so can we. Let me mention only three instances I happen to know of personally, from among the hundreds that are signs of this new situation: the *Soirée Ecumenique* at the Faith and Order Conference at Montreal last summer (when Cardinal Léger joined Orthodox and Protestant leaders in a memorable and moving service of common prayer and fellowship); a similar service in San Antonio, where Bishop Leven joined one Episcopalian and two Methodist bishops in an ecumenical assembly that continues to have significant repercussions throughout that region; and, finally, the service in the North Carolina mountains last August when Archbishop Hallinan addressed an important conference sponsored by the World Methodist Council and laid before us a tremendous challenge of mutual endeavor in the cause of Christian unity. Such a list could be extended on and on of incidents that you know better than I.

What has happened is that the first great miracle of the ecumenical reality has been wrought in our midst— and who will deny that this is God's doing and marvelous in our eyes? It is the miracle of our mutual recognition of each other as Christians, as sharing, somehow and in some degree, both in Word and Sacrament, in the saving mystery of the People of God, wherein God in Christ "has transferred us from the kingdom of darkness into the kingdom of his beloved Son, in whom we have redemption, the forgiveness of sins" (Col. 1:13-14). It is the miracle of our mutual acknowledgment of our God-given unity in Christ and of our mutual participation in the supreme Christian Tradition (which is the self-givenness of God in the self-giving of Jesus Christ, for us men and for our salvation) despite the variety and contrariety of our ecclesiastical *traditiones et consuetudines*.

But we are also aware that these are only the first fruits of this council in the current ecumenical epoch. None of us presumes—nor do we suppose that any of you does, either—that *communicatio in sacris* is within sight or even in early prospect. We are agreed, I take it, that this is not to be sought or proffered at the price of compromise on your part or abjuration on ours. It is painfully clear that yet *another* miracle will be required before the whole pilgrim People of God is visibly united as the *one* People of God, the one household of faith. But the miracles and charisms we have already witnessed in our time in this ecumenical age, and in this ecumenical council, bolster our faith that this is indeed the time in which our Lord means for his separated brethren to obey his manifest will *ut omnes unum sint!*

In the interim, however, there is a formidable budget of work that must be undertaken, some of it together and some of it separately. For us, your "separated brethren," there is the task of discovering and appraising the richness of the treasures of the deposit of faith which you have conserved and served in the course of the tragic centuries of our separation. You must realize (and not be offended by it) that the burden of our reservations toward you, from both Orthodox and Protestant sides, has not been that Rome is *too* catholic, but rather not *catholic* enough. It is as you actually manifest your real catholicity and as we discover and share in it that we shall be moved forward toward that eventual convergence that will be unity.

On your side, if it be not impertinent to suggest such a thing, your obedience to the Spirit's command to unity would seem to require a truly radical renewal of your own ancient tradition of the prime authority of the Word of God in Scripture, with its grand themes of God's utter sovereignty and grace, of man's justification and sanctification through God's sheer, unmerited gift in Christ, of God's solemn judgment against all *latreia* of any creature, all celestialism and triumphalism in church history.

It is also worth remarking that, from our point of view, your working definition of ecumenism (as expressed in chapter one of the *Decree on Ecumenism*) is valid enough as far as it goes, but is patently incomplete. In it, you recognize, in good faith and full charity, the ecclesial and soteriological realities in the *ecclesiae vel communitates* not now in communion with you. This is clearly the essential presupposition of any and all honest ecumenism. But have you an adequate *theory* to account for such ecumenical actualities? How can such things be—with what doctrinal warrant—with what ecclesiological consequences? Your answers to these questions will be decisive as to what can be done now, or ever, to transcend our tragic and bitter histories of schism and mutual recrimination. It so happens, of course—and we have just begun to realize it ourselves—that by tackling the question in the *Constitution on the Church*, you are putting real pressure on *us* to risk similar experiments in self-examination and reform. Such experiments are actually going forward in our various Churches and church families and in the World Council of Churches. But it still bears mentioning that one of the most effective stimuli to ecclesiastical reform in modern Christendom is coming from the Church that we once thought to be unreformed and irreformable.

In the days and years before us, we are under a clear mandate from our one and common Lord to continue in this uneasy dialogue between separated brethren who rejoice in the reality of our being *brethren* (and brethren in Christ!). Yet we grieve over the stark realities of our being separated by honest clashes of convictions as to the substance of the Christian faith and the essence of the Christian life. In this dialogue—made all the more difficult now that it has become so open and honest—we would do well to keep in mind the wise counsel of Pope Paul VI to the monks of St. Nilus' Abbey at Grottaferrata last August:

We are all a little hard of hearing; we are all a little slow of speech. May the Lord enable us to hear each others' voices, the voices of history, the voices of the saints, his own voice, which is still our Law and Power.

Something strange and wonderful is happening in the Roman Catholic Church today, of which this council is both sign and effectual agent. You have, or so it seems to some of us, closed the chapter of your history that was entitled "Counter-Reformation" and have begun the first draft of a new chapter that has as its tentative title, "Reformation and Renewal." If you succeed in getting *this* chapter written—or even sketched out—in this council, it will not only alter the visage of the Church of Rome but will warm the heart of the whole of Christendom. In this way, you can open the way, not only to a new plenitude of catholicity in the People of God, but you can help greatly in bringing that People into an even more effective obedience to Christ's great commission and promise: "Go ye therefore into all the world and disciple all nations . . ." (Mt. 28:19).

This is why in these days, there is no group in the *aula* of St. Peter's, or anywhere else in the world, more attentive, more concerned, or more hopeful than those of us in the tribune beneath St. Longinus' spear!

CHAPTER 4

VATICANUM SECUNDUM:
TWO COUNCILS IN ONE

December 28, 1963

One of the items on the program of the annual meeting of the American Historical Association is a joint session with the American Society of Church History. On December 28, 1963, this session was devoted to the first and second Vatican Councils. I had just returned from Rome, after session two of Vatican II. The following paper is, therefore, an historian's attempt to rehearse for other historians the salient features of the council as church history in the making. Their uncommon interest in the topic was evident by an unusually large attendance and their probing questions.

Such papers always have appointed critics. Mine on this occasion was Professor James Hastings Nichols of Princeton Theological Seminary [author of *Democracy and the Churches*, Westminster Press, 1951; *Primer for Protestants*, Association Press, 1947] who had attended session one as a delegated-observer of the Presbyterian World Alliance and was well-known as one of Rome's dourest detractors. He pitched into the paper zestfully as fatuously over-optimistic in its estimate of the council's commitment to reform. The ensuing exchange was livelier than most at such gatherings. What is interesting about this, though, is that the subsequent history has proved us both wrong—Nichols in his skepticism, I in my caution. But this is only another instance where the council has confounded the historians.

The audience for this essay were professional historians, hard-nosed, rigorous and largely secularist—yet also intensely curious about the phenomenon of a great Church involved in a massive experiment in self-criticism and self-understanding. The title referred to the fact that the council, which had been launched by one Pope, had been resumed by his successor—with portents and consequences then still far from clear.

At the moment, Vatican II is very much *in medias res*—and now stands at a highly critical juncture in its development as a council. Moreover, it is an incredibly complicated phenomenon, a veritable quicksilver subject for reliable assessment. The historian's difficulties are further complicated because it has become the most widely publicized event in church history. The imaginations of the journalists, ecclesiastical and secular, have been fired (in hope or horror) by the prospect of drastic and dramatic changes in the posture and direction of the Roman Catholic Church—and many of them have been led to see the council as a sort of ecclesiastical horse opera, with "good guys" and "bad guys," heroes and villains—*Gunsmoke* in St. Peter's. They are busy people, the journalists in Rome, but for all too many of them, their prime project is to zero in on the buried bodies thereabouts. With very few exceptions, the journalists I talked to (a small army of them) were more interested in the council's *conflicts* than in its *processes*. They were either indifferent to, or uncomprehending of, the theological and pastoral concerns that had convoked the council and are its real justification. Thus, the most interesting reports—e.g., Rynne's in *The New Yorker*, Kaiser's in *Time*, Fesquet's in *Le Monde*—remind me of nothing so much as Robert Browne's *Treatise of Reformation Without Tarrying for Any* . . . (1582)—save that Browne's rhetoric is pretty

44

dismal, whereas his modern avatars (Catholics, too, they are) could write the script for *Bonanza*. None of this would matter very much were it not that their misleading stereotypes appear to be convincing a great many people: that, for example, the council, conceived by the good Pope John and launched under highly favorable auspices and omens, has now finally bogged down, sabotaged by those villains in the Roman curia; or that the will of the majority of the bishops is being thwarted—and may finally be defeated—by the Holy Office; or that Pope Paul (on whom such high hopes had been pinned at first) has turned out to be a Hamlet-like creature, weakly halting before two unwelcome options: to be, or not to be, a strong pope? One problem in revising these stereotypes stems from the fact that there is just enough substance in each to lend them the lure of fascinating half-truths.

The plan for an ecumenical council was first announced by Pope John XXIII on January 25, 1959. The ante-preparatory commissions actually got down to real business in May, 1960. The first session of the council began on October 11, 1962, and ran through December 8. The second session was convened on September 29, 1963, and adjourned on December 4. There have been 79 working sessions—"general congregations"—(36 in the first session; 43 in the second). Something more than one-half million episcopal man-hours have been already spent in these general congregations alone. To this must be added almost as much again to cover their time in commission meetings, episcopal conferences, press conferences, etc., etc. Finally, one has to add on the lavish outlay of talent and energy by the battalions of *periti* and the squads of *observatores* and *auditores*. When it comes to an estimate of the financial cost of it all, a frugal man simply shudders!

Now, what is there to show for all this? What credence

belongs to all the brave talk we have heard of renovation and reform? It is at this point that the apostles of impatience begin to groan or to jibe. The formal results are meager:

1. *A Message to the World* (dated October 21, 1962) which is significant chiefly because of its authorship (Liénart, Doepfner, Alfrink, Suenens) and because in it the theme of episcopal collegiality was sounded *before* it has been raised as an explicit issue in the council.

2. A papal *motu proprio* (*Pastorales Munus*, December 3, 1963) restoring a modest block of "privileges and powers" hitherto reserved to Rome back to the diocesan bishops.

3. Two promulgated documents (December 4, 1963)—the *Constitution on the Sacred Liturgy* and the *Decree on the Media of Social Communications.* The former of these is an impressive demonstration of what a fully considered, repeatedly revised conciliar schema can be, a major forward step with immense consequences. As for the mass media decree, it is a sample of conciliar haste—three and one-half days debate last fall, with 56 interventions; no discussion at all in the second session. On the weekend before final vote in congregation (November 25, 1963) there was a flurry of agitation against the schema and denunciations of it as woefully inadequate. These criticisms were valid enough, but they ignored the pressure that had been put on the bishops—in part by the journalists!—to get something done to show for their efforts.

This, then, is the council's dilemma: if it hurries, its results are bound to be inferior. If it takes the necessary time to ventilate an issue and to revise and re-revise the texts, people complain of its bogging down.

This is why it seems important to recognize that the main thing happening at Rome is a massive experiment in self-examination and *aggiornamento,* carried forward by a very large, very unwieldy, very conservative institution. Moreover, this experiment is being undertaken with a deep and sincere concern to bring off its reforms *without* the cruelties of a heresy hunt or the scars of a schism. Given the heritage of bitterness between Rome and Eastern Orthodoxy (1054, 1204, Florence[1]), given the inbuilt defensiveness of the Church of the Counter-Reformation and the Risorgimento, given the dangers of plunging such an institution into the ideological maelstrom of modern, anti-supernaturalistic world-views, who should have expected that *aggiornamento* would come easily, or that basic changes in perspective and polity would happen overnight—or even over-year?

And yet a basic change of climate has begun to take place in the Roman Catholic Church—chiefly as a consequence of this council. Judgments may differ as to how far the metamorphosis has gone; prognostications disagree as to how far it will get. The essential point, to date, is that the venture is being pushed with a clear awareness of the stakes involved. Matched against the needs of the time, or the hunger of the contemporary Christian heart for authentic Christian unity, it can easily be said that Vatican II has not yet achieved what its advocates hoped for it, or believed was possible. Nor may it ever. But, judged in the light of other councils and other experiments in

[1] Three of the crises in the history of the estrangements between Rome and Constantinople. 1054: the mutual excommunications of the Patriarch and the Pope rescinded and annulled at the close of Vatican II. 1204: the sack of Constantinople by the Crusaders, a savage blow that fatally weakened the city's power to resist the besieging Moslems. The Council of Florence (1438-45) achieved a formal act of reunion between the Pope and Patriarch which was promptly repudiated by the Orthodox and voided by the fall of Constantinople to Mahomet the Conqueror. Even today, the memories of these events rankle in the hearts of the Orthodox and complicate every venture in reconciliation.

47

ecclesiastical reforms—or seen against the background of its own prehistory—it seems only honest and fair to judge that Vatican II has already achieved an extraordinary success. Even if no more is accomplished than what we now have—the reform of the liturgy, the establishment of the principle of episcopal collegiality and the commitment of the Roman Catholic Church to a vital program of ecumenism—Vatican II will have to be recorded as an epoch-making event.

As we all know, Vatican I was adjourned (1870) with a very large budget of unfinished business. It is often implied that if *that* council had been resumed, its *dogmata* on papal primacy and infallibility would have been balanced by a definition of episcopal collegiality. This is certainly wrong. The whole course of Vatican I was a triumph for an ancient feudal mind-set in doctrine, discipline and polity. If, thereafter, the Roman dicasteries were able to push their role as papal surrogates, it was without any strong or principled dissent from hierarchy or laity around the world. Nothing about Vatican I can be called "progressive." Moreover, one of its side-effects was to render the notion of a later council redundant. This view became commonplace—which is why Pope John's proposal was so surprising.

The unchallenged acceptance of papal absolutism had developed as a reaction to the persistent aggregates of the Church's feudal past, the scars of ceaseless church-state struggles throughout the whole of European history right down to modern times, the collisions of the *Syllabus of Errors* (1864) with "modernism" in its myriad forms. Whatever one's estimate of the wisdom or folly of committing the Roman Catholic Church to a real encounter with modernity, it should be recognized that the positive effort of today's traditionalists is to prevent the disasters that they believe are inevitable consequences of this *aggiornamento* of which the progressives speak so glibly.

The strength of their case lies in their conviction that the doctrines of Trent and of Vatican I are indefectible and irreversible. From this, it follows for them that Vatican I settled, once and for all, the questions of papal primacy and infallibility. It also means that the papal dicasteries share in the papal absolutism and are consequently omnicompetent. This is what Cardinal Ottaviani had in mind when he reminded Cardinal Frings that the *Pope* was the head of the Holy Office and that any criticism of said Holy Office was criticism of the Pope—which comes close to equating Pope Paul and Cardinal Ottaviani. Thus, the traditionalists had concluded that the Pope was fully authorized to govern the Church directly with or without a council, with or without the consensus of "the episcopal college," *if any*. This was their exegesis of that fateful last sentence of Vatican I's decree on infallibility: *ideoque ejusmodi Romani Pontificis definitiones ex sese, non autem ex consensu ecclesiae [vel hierarchiae], irreformabiles esse*. A council was at best unnecessary and at worst a threat to "the perfect society" already realized in Rome.

It is highly significant that not a single "progressive" has thus far dared even to hint that the *Syllabus of Errors* or the *Pastor Aeternus* of Vatican I requires amendment in any respect whatever. Ironically, it is this dilemma of trying to reform the irreformable without advertising it that prompts Rome's critics and cynics to doubt that it will ever really change and to insinuate that what some of us suppose are signs of change are mere illusions. Incidentally, these doubts and insinuations, expressed in various ways by Protestant critics (including some of the observers!), are beginning to rasp a bit on the sensitive nerve endings of some of the Roman ecumenists. They are also being noted with unconcealed smugness by the Roman traditionalists—and one notices striking psychological similarities in the immobilist spirit on *both* sides!

Here, then, is the problem posed by Vatican II—and other such projects in church renewal: can established religious institutions reform themselves, or be reformed, without schism, on the one hand, or recidivism on the other? Nobody knows, really—for church history has been discouraging on this point, so far. But it does seem to me a mite self-righteous for the Orthodox (who oppose reform on principle!) and the Protestants (who proudly advocate the *principle* of reform, at whatever cost of schism *and* recidivism) to denigrate the tremendous and deliberate effort at renovation which Vatican II represents.

What the Roman traditionalists had not reckoned with was the vision and passion of a Pope who had spent very little of his ministry in Rome, who had already been something of a one-man ecumenical movement in Sofia, Istanbul and Paris, and who retained the residues of his early training at Bergamo under mildly modernist influences. By the same token, Pope John had not reckoned with the extent of the actual control of the papal office wielded by the Roman curia. It was the shock of *this* recognition, more than anything else, that prompted him to project a council. This, more than anything else, accounts for those stories about raised windows and Pope John's alleged complaint: *"Io sono nel sacco qui."* Thus the council became for him a complex of means toward a whole syndrome of ends: (1) personal maneuver room for the Pope himself who, with his fellow bishops gathered about him, could alter the structures and functions of the power structures in the Church; (2) a collective endeavor in re-evaluating the nature and mission of the Church; (3) a crucial test case in putting the theory of episcopal collegiality into practice.

Thus, Vatican II is John XXIII's council—pre-eminently in the first session but no less really in the second. One of the really great moments of both sessions (and intended as such!) came with Pope Paul's commemoration of the *fifth* anniversary of Pope John's election (October 28, 1958). The night before, I asked Msgr. Jan Willebrands (secretary of the Secretariat for Promoting Christian Unity) if the Pope would celebrate mass in the council *aula* (in the midst of the bishops) or at the high altar (reserved to him alone). I got an interesting answer: "In the *aula,* if 'they' will let him." "They" did let him and he did celebrate at the low altar in the *aula* and personally served communion to the *auditores.* He then introduced the eulogist (Leo Joseph Cardinal Suenens of Malines-Brussels) who proceeded in one of the best speeches of either session to stress the continuity of the two councils—John's *and* Paul's—and to chart the road ahead in unmistakably progressive terms. This was done with the obvious approval of Paul VI, beaming from his chair beneath Bernini's baldochino.

At *this* distance, it is too easily forgotten that the original call to council caught the Church flat-footed—lacking both conciliar experience and a proper doctrine of the conciliar process. I have seen a part of the mountain of memoranda with which the bishops flooded the preparatory commissions—which then undertook to focus this vast jumble and to prepare schemas which the bishops could debate and vote on. The least that one can say of *that* task—given its background and circumstances—is that it involved the reconciliation of the irreconcilable. Moreover, at that stage no one knew or could even rightly guess at the relative strengths of the various tendencies within the various segments of the episcopate as a whole —how the critical issues that would be raised in the council could possibly be resolved. Here, as elsewhere, one shakes a wondering head at the confidence with which Pope John risked so much, so impulsively, to the charismatic presence of the Holy Spirit in the council.

The most illuminating way I know to construe the successive crises of session one is to see them as so many steps in the process by which the bishops began to get the hang and habit of *acting as an episcopal college!* The crucial moment came at the very outset. During the first fifteen minutes of the very first general congregation (October 13, 1962) a successful effort was made to have a free election of the members of the commissions who would produce the conciliar documents. In the place of the rigged slate presented by the curia, the bishops proceeded to elect representative commissions! The experiment in episcopal collegiality was then continued in the protracted debate on the liturgy (October 21-November 15). Dull as this seemed to some, it may now be seen as truly indispensable for any significant consensus on the spirit and substance of liturgical reform. One has only to compare the first, intermediate and *final* texts of the *Constitution on the Sacred Liturgy* in order to realize the decisive importance of that debate. This developing experience of collegiality reached its climax in session one on November 20, when a motion to reject the proposed schema on the sources of Revelation was put and lost—by a margin of only 78 votes less than the two-thirds majority required for rejection (for: 1,368; against: 822). This proved —and the point had been in doubt up to that moment— that the progressives were in a *substantial* majority, but not an *overwhelming* one. Pope John then swiftly proceeded to rescue the bishops from their dilemma by a unilateral papal action. I've a notion that Pope Paul would have let the bishops stew in their collegial juices a while longer. This, at least, is what he seems to be doing now.

Pope John never lived to see even the first fruits of his vision—and may never have fully realized what he was letting the Church in for. But the validity of his charism was confirmed in the crisp determination of the cardinals to elect a successor who would continue the council. When Giovanni-Battista Montini, Cardinal Archbishop of Milan, was elected on June 21, 1963 (on the third day of the conclave) , three inferences were obvious:

1. That this new Pope owed his election to a *coalition* of traditionalists and progressives—since the latter could not have mustered the requisite majority. This meant that the liberals trusted Montini to continue to press for Roncalli's goals; it also meant that the conservatives expected no less, but trusted him to proceed in his reforms with due regard for the papal establishment (since he was himself a veteran of it) .
2. That the council would resume; that its procedures would be reorganized; that the center of concern in the forthcoming session would be *ecclesiology.*
3. That the hinge of the schema on the Church would be the issue of *episcopal collegiality,* since this had been conceived of as the chief means to the practical reform of the Church at large.

And so it has transpired. On September 21, eight days before the second session convened, the new Pope gracefully informed the curia that they had two choices: they could reform *themselves,* or they could *be* reformed. In his first allocution to the council as Pope (September 29), he introduced himself to his fellow bishops as the head of the episcopal college and then charted the main objectives of the continuing council in four points: "the self-understanding of the Church; its reform; the bringing together of all Christians in unity; the dialogue of the Church with the contemporary world." He went on to speak frankly of *renovatio,* of the imperfections of the Church which "belong to the infirmities of being human," of the possibilities of diversity in Christian unity and, in a climax of great feeling, he proposed *mutual* repentance and forgiveness "for the grief endured during our long sequence of dissensions and separations." He concluded with a counsel against any "solemn dogmatic definitions" which might harden the lines of present divisions.

Thereafter, his "presence" in the council was constant but always indirect. I got the impression, not of a Hamlet, but of a Lincoln—a highly reflective leader who favors reforms but is reluctant to impose them, *par force majeure*. He seems to regard collegiality as the right pattern of leadership in the Church, and so he refuses to stultify that principle by resolving differences within the *collegium episcoporum* by papal fiat! That *this* should be complained of by those who pose as advocates of reform seems faintly ironic.

I wish there were time to describe the weird fashion, as it seemed to me, in which the council's business is conducted. The agenda is largely improvised, almost from day to day—never much more than that. Announcements—and even votes—are sprung on the fathers on scandalously short notice (in terms of Roberts' *Rules of Order*, at least!) and all this while the "interventions" proceed relentlessly from about 9:30 (after mass) until noon (the angelus). The point is that only the most nimble-witted ever quite know what is going on or what is coming up. This clearly tended to encourage compliance with the management—and this is clearly the management's intent.

It is agreed on all sides that if the principle of collegiality is finally and explicitly affirmed, the result will be a drastic dispersal of episcopal leadership throughout the world (through the augmented responsibilities of regional or territorial conferences, etc.). It seems further agreed that such a collegiate episcopate would move the Roman Catholic Church into the future far more swiftly and forthrightly than ever the Mediterraneans would dare. What is in dispute is whether or not such a move is **wise or reckless**. It is on this judgment that the issue of *aggiornamento* turns, more than any other. This is the disagreement that has brought the council to its deepest crisis.

In making a chart of the speakers on collegiality one is struck by the homogeneity of the background of the 31 fathers who *opposed* the idea. Twenty-six were from *two* countries. Fifteen were Italians, 11 were Spaniards, two Frenchmen (both *curialisti*), one Ukrainian, one Brazilian. Number 31 in the list was Michael Cardinal Browne, of Ireland—Master-General of the Dominicans —*curialista* and arch-traditionalist. It was Browne who ended his impassioned defense of the standing order by shaking a bony finger at the bishops and shouting down the *aula: "Venerabiles patres,* CAVEAMUS!" On the other side, there were 52 speakers from 25 countries—many of them representing episcopal *blocs* in their countries, or linguistic areas. Ten were French, seven German, three Americans. There were only two Spaniards and only two Italians: Cardinal-President Siri and Bishop Betazzi, auxiliary of Bologna—who got a hearty round of applause for his non-conformity. He maintained that collegiality had been recognized as a legitimate view by the medieval *curialisti* and canonists—it was *not* a Gallican or transalpine "invention."

On October 15, the moderator of the day, Cardinal Suenens, announced that there would be a straw vote on the main issues as they had been defined in the course of the debate on chapter two of the *Constitution on the Church* (collegiality). This move was promptly contested as *ultra vires* by the general secretary, Archbishop Pericle Felici, whom the observers have nicknamed "Uncle Pericles," because of his avuncular ways of telling off his fellow bishops. Felici was supported by several of the cardinal-presidents. After a fierce backstage struggle, the moderators carried their point—and on October 30 there came a vote fully as critical as that of the preceding November 20. It took the form of four queries carefully formulated in an ascending order of explicit stress:

1. "Whether it would please the fathers for the schema to state that episcopal consecration constitutes the highest grade of the sacrament of orders?" To this query, there were 2,123 *placets* (98.49 percent).

2. "Whether it would please the fathers for the schema to state that every bishop legitimately consecrated, in communion with the other bishops and with the Roman pontiff as their head and principle of unity, is thereby made a member of the *corpus episcoporum?*" To this, 2,049 voted "yes" (95.12 percent).

3. "Whether it would please the fathers that the schema should state that, in its tasks of evangelizing, sanctifying and feeding, the body or college of bishops succeeds the college of the apostles; and that, in union with its head, the Roman pontiff (and never without this head, whose primatial rights[2] remain intact), this *corpus episcoporum* enjoys full and supreme authority over the universal church?" Here was the doctrine full-blown; and yet it got 1,808 *placets* (84.18 percent).

4. "Whether it would please the fathers for the schema to state that the aforesaid power belongs to the *collegium episcoporum* (united with its *caput*) by *divine right?*" This was number three above, doubled in spades (with that *ius divinum!*) and yet it got 1,717 *placets* (80.80 percent).

A fifth ballot, on the restoration of a permanent diaconate, went 74.95 percent in the affirmative, 187 votes more than the required two-thirds majority. One might have supposed that this settled the matter. But Ottaviani, Ruf-

---

[2] Cardinal Bacci wanted this to read "rights as primate" and made quite an issue of the difference!

fini, Browne and Bacci—wheelhorses on the theological commission—promptly served notice that no such *suffragium indicativum* was decisive for them! The procedure was irregular, the questions loaded and the results supportive of error—which must not be countenanced even if advocated by an overwhelming majority of the bishops.

Then followed a long series of maneuvers, curiously climaxed by a further *collegial election* of additional members of the commissions—including the theological commission. This ballot (November 28) was yet another signal "victory" for the progressives: the 42 new men came from 29 different countries, with only one Italian and two Spaniards in the lot. There were six Americans (seven, if you count Bishop John Taylor of Stockholm, Sweden). Thus, once again, as in every other explicit test of the council's mind, the results are consistent and plain: *given a choice,* this council intends to end the Mediterranean hegemony in the Roman Catholic Church! From now until final action on the *Constitution on the Church—* and also the *Decree on the Pastoral Office of the Bishops in the Church*—watch for what happens to the doctrine now approved by those four *utrums* of last October. No other calculus of the council's prospects will be more accurate or revealing.

Four other significant items from the second session may be mentioned in hasty conclusion. The first was the debate on the *Decree on Ecumenism*. This was remarkable for its four accent points: 1. the explicit recognition of the "separated brethren" as *Christian* brethren, by virtue of their baptism and their confession of faith in Jesus Christ (thereby mooting the thorny question of schismatic or heretical baptism!); 2. the affirmation of the principle of unity-in-diversity as the authentic catholic view of Christian community; 3. a categorical repudiation of any *especial* guilt of the Jews in the death of Jesus (thereby scuttling an ancient slander); 4. a rousing declaration of the rights of conscience in matters of faith and religious practice (thereby registering the lessons learned by the Roman Catholics from their North American experience).

A second item is related to these final chapters on religious liberty and on the Jews, and it makes a strange story. On November 21, the fathers were informed that the discussion *in specie* of the *Decree on Ecumenism* would be confined to chapters one through three. At a later date (*in proximis diebus*), said Felici, separate votes would be taken on the last two chapters. The bishops agreed, most of them supposing that *in proximis diebus* meant "in a few days"—that is, *before* the adjournment of the current session. There was, in fact, a deal between Cardinal Bea and the council management to this effect. How and why this deal was ditched is something of a "whodunit." It involved the convulsive reaction of the Mediterranean hierarchies against the practical and political effects of the doctrine of religious liberty (including strong pleas from the leaders of the Christian Democratic Party in Italy that action be deferred until after the Italian elections next July). There were, besides, strong reactions from the Roman Catholic Uniates in Arab countries against a friendly word from the council to the Jews (reinforced by stern threats from the governments of the Arab countries). Finally, there were the misgivings of a fair number of theologians (otherwise in favor of the doctrines in both chapters) as to the honest logic of tacking these topics, as they stand, onto the *Decree on Ecumenism*, as it stands.

The atmosphere got pretty tense during the final week of the session. Would there be any action on chapters four and five? Would they get lost in the interim between session two and session three (as many suspected the opposition intended)? When and how would the promise, *in proximis diebus,* be redeemed, if ever? What actually happened *in public* came on December 2 (general congregation 79). Cardinal Bea read a low-keyed statement, expressing the disappointment of his Secretariat that chapters four and five had not been considered, *in specie,* but assuring the bishops that they would be up for discussion early on in the third session. There the matter stands, as of the moment—and its further development bears a very close watch. There will, of course, be resolute efforts to suppress them, or to render them innocuous. But it is most unlikely that any such hanky-panky will prevail, for the bishops have now discovered something of their powers and responsibilities—and they will not take a second double-cross lying down.

The third item, of course, was the approval and promulgation of the *Constitution on the Sacred Liturgy.* The simplest thing to say about this is that it is at once the charter for a major mutation in the patterns of worship of Roman Catholics the world over *and* the first major test of episcopal collegiality in action—since the responsibility for implementing these changes lies with the bishops, in their several dioceses and episcopal conferences. Several of the avant-garde liturgists have complained that the schema as promulgated was a mere half-loaf. However, when one rehearses the history of liturgical reform since Lateran IV (1215) and considers the radical effects in corporate religion that always follow basic changes in ritual practices, it seems hard to doubt that the *Constitution on the Sacred Liturgy* has, in fact, committed the Roman Catholic Church to a tremendous enterprise of *aggiornamento* in one of the most vital areas of its life.

Our final item concerns the *Decree on the Instruments of Social Communication.* The truth is that many of those who voted for that decree did so without enthusiasm. Its most apparent fault is that parts of it can be abused by reactionaries claiming rights of *censorship* in the name of that holy ambiguity, "the common good." A more complex appraisal of it might, however, add three other points: 1. the decree does take cognizance of the fact that the technology of mass communications is here to stay; 2. it does provide a challenge and opportunity to update the communicative processes in a Church that has cherished privacy more than most; 3. inadequate as it is, the decree marks a step beyond the laggard progress in some other religious communities in this same field. The *major* moral I find in this instance is that this council has been wholly unprepared to conclude any of its issues thus far without a very elaborate process of reflection, debate, revision and re-revision.

The third session of Vatican II is now scheduled to convene next mid-September, to run through mid-November. Meanwhile we must bear in mind that *the Council-in-*RECESS *continues as the Council-in-*PROCESS. When I took my leave of our hosts at the Secretariat on the afternoon of December 4, they were already hard at work collating some four or five hundred *modi* already received for the next revision of the *Decree on Ecumenism* for session three and were expecting half as many more before the deadline for amendments (February 1). The ceaseless intrigue and gossip in Rome and the Vatican goes on and on—but so also does the ferment of self-examination among the bishops, priests and layfolk around the world. One can sense that many bishops are developing a very much stronger sense of responsibility for the management and program of the council than they had brought with them last year, or even last September. *This* seems to me especially true of the North Americans. Thus, it seems likely that their influence in matters of strategy will increase as time goes on. This means, as I see it, that the traditionalists will be unable to maintain the seemingly impregnable tactical position they began with four years ago. Still and all, the balances are precarious, the parallelogram of forces is exceedingly complex, the future is genuinely uncertain.

It is true, of course, that an historian, with his blasé recollections of all the thwarted and aborted reforms across the ages, is reflexively skeptical of any glib prediction that the Roman Catholic Church can achieve a really thoroughgoing and abiding *renovatio* here and now. But his skepticism is merely doctrinaire (or even pathological) if he fails to appreciate the magnitude of the efforts already put forth, the sincerity of motives and spirit among the participants, the excitements that have followed the collapse of the old ghetto walls that have kept Christian brethren apart. He is simply obtuse if he ignores the manifest determination of the majority of the Roman Catholic episcopate—and Pope Paul with them as their head!—to realize as much of John's dream as falls inside the scope of historical possibility.

Thus even if the millennium does not burst on us next autumn—or even the one thereafter—the Christian world is already a great deal better off for the experience of Vatican II. And, always supposing that renewal in *any* part of the Body of Christ contributes to the health of the whole Body, we may all have much more still to be grateful for in the work of this council before it is over and done.

CHAPTER 5

WHAT IF VATICAN II SUCCEEDS?

May, 1964

From the beginning, I had been deeply concerned about the negative reactions to the council which kept cropping up here and there among the Protestants, some of them prominently identified with the ecumenical movement at one level or another. It was one thing, it seemed to me, to maintain one's principled objections to this theological position or that ecclesiastic polity and quite another to reject on bias the possibility of authentic reform in the Roman Catholic Church as such. Prejudgments like this were an offense against charity— a sort of *Protestant* triumphalism in reverse! Besides, they tended to weaken the cause of reform by confirming the Roman *immobilisti* in *their* prejudices that openness toward Protestants was futile anyhow.

When, therefore (in January, 1964), an invitation came from our Methodist student magazine, *Motive,* to do a short piece for them on the council, I decided to comment in public on this phenomenon of Protestant immobilism—to a student audience on whose sympathy I could count. Pope Paul's pilgrimage to Palestine had come off well; the initial reactions to the *Constitution on the Sacred Liturgy* had been generally favorable; support for the progressive cause was growing in America; the interest of the world in the council continued high. On all these grounds, the prospects of "success" were better than ever. On the other hand, none of the crucial reform issues (besides the liturgy) had been settled; the opposition was still zealous and powerful; there was a sizable bloc of uncommitted bishops who might, for all we knew then, go either way. And, above all, the policy of Paul VI was still ambiguous enough to allow for widely varying estimates of his commitments. As of that date, it was far from certain that Vatican II *would* succeed.

The following article, written in February and published in *Motive* in May, 1964, was, therefore, a slender essay in prophecy and a mild chiding of some of my brethren for their anti-Roman biases. If Vatican II had faltered, it would have left me with a very red face, a minor casualty in a major disaster. As it turned out, the council has made my "daring" prophecy seem curiously cautious in retrospect. But, the main point—that the "success" of Vatican II poses a major challenge to Protestantism—is still valid, and now even more exigent than before.

Only a cynic can any longer doubt that Vatican II represents a major effort at basic reform and renewal in the Roman Catholic Church. Pope John XXIII made this clear in his convocation of the council—as also with his slogan of *aggiornamento* ("bringing the Church up to date"). Pope Paul VI reiterated this same theme, with variations, in his opening address to the *second* session (his first as Pope):

. . . For reasons of brevity and better understanding, we enumerate here the four main objectives of this council in four points: the self-understanding of the Church; its reform; the bringing together of all Christians in unity; the dialogue of the Church with the contemporary world. . . .

The reform at which the council is aiming is not a turning upside down of the Church's present way of life nor a breaking with what is essential in her tradition. Rather, it is the honoring of that tradition by stripping from it what is defective so that it may become more firm and fruitful.

These words were subsequently echoed and reechoed, in St. Peter's and in the Catholic press, by leaders and followers, in a mounting chorus. It is an instance of mass deception on a very large scale if reform and renewal have not become both the passion and the hope of a great multitude of Roman Catholics around the world—except, of course, in "the Mediterranean segment" of that world.

By the same token Vatican II is also a major experiment in ecumenicity. Already the traditional Roman policy of aloofness (reaffirmed as recently as 1928 by Pius XI in *Mortalium Animos*) has begun to shift about to a genuine openness. One evidence of this reversal is the establishment of a permanent Secretariat for Promoting Christian Unity; another, the welcoming into the council itself of a sizable corps of non-Catholic "observers." Yet another is the general and genuine acknowledgment of us "separated brethren" as *Christian* brethren. Concern for Christian unity was the strongest single motivation for the Pope's pilgrimage to Palestine. There cannot be many places left, in the United States at least, where the basic change in the ecumenical "weather patterns" in Catholic-Protestant relationships has gone unregistered.

All this being so, one would think that those who regard reform as a constant, vital principle in the life of the ongoing Church (and who are professed advocates of Christian unity) would find in Vatican II a ground of rejoicing and high hopes. And so they have—many of them. It is not merely for its fuss and feathers that Vatican II is the most widely publicized event in the entire history of the Christian Church. It is all too true that there are many ardent—and some naive—optimists who refuse to recognize the enormous difficulties involved. They expect too much, too soon, too easily. This way lies disenchantment. Yet, even so, there is a vast company in the world (and not just Christians, either) who have perceived (if only dimly) that if Vatican II *succeeds*, the consequences may well be wonderful for the Christian community and for the world besides.

It is something of a scandal, therefore, that so many non-Roman reactionaries should have joined their Roman counterparts in viewing the conciliar experiment in reform with skepticism and suspicion. It was to have been expected that the diehards in the Roman curia would have to be dragged over the thresholds of change. This is the normal fate of fossils. On the other side, it has also been natural enough for the Protestant fundamentalists to stand firm in their loud detestations of the pope as "that antichrist, that man of sin and son of perdition" (to quote the amiable words of the *Westminster Confession*, XXV, vi).

But it still raises my eyebrows to discover what looks like an implacable anti-Roman bias among veteran ecumenists of experience and stature. It was a prominent member of the Faith and Order Commission of the World Council of Churches who, in a recent "ecumenical" handbook, asserted bluntly: "All we can rightly learn from Rome is how *not* to be the Church." It was the "business committee" of the Fourth World Conference on Faith and Order in Montreal last summer that beat down first a proposal for a fraternal message from our Conference to Vatican II—and then an even more innocuous motion that we send greetings to the Secretariat for Promoting Christian Unity. It was a group of prominent European Protestants (leaders in the World Council of Churches) who, in Rome last fall, offended many liberal Catholics with their allegations of insincerity and self-deception in the council—and then *boycotted* the public session held in commemoration of the Council of Trent (December 3, 1963).

It was an American "observer" who, last December before the American Historical Association, denounced the Church of Rome as an incorrigible papal absolutism, all protestations to the contrary notwithstanding. Is it possible that such men are still so bitter about their ancient enmities that they will be *glad* if Vatican II *fails?*

Still, bias has its uses. In this case, these bigoted reactions remind us that, if Vatican II *succeeds,* it will drastically upset the standing order in the contemporary Christian community. Both Protestants and Orthodox Christians would then be confronted with an urgent and undeclinable challenge to reform their own ranks, or else! It will be a strange new world, indeed, if it is a reformed Church of Rome that forces the wrangling fragments of non-Roman Christendom to face up to the scandal of "our unhappy divisions" and to risk a genuine *aggiornamento* of our own. And yet the Romans have already captured the initiative in the ecumenical movement and, at least for the time being, are setting the pace in the ecumenical dialogue (with the World Council of Churches in one of its periodic slumps).

As just one example, consider what will happen to us Protestants as the new *Constitution on the Sacred Liturgy* opens the way for radical liturgical reform among our Catholic brethren—with the result that their worship may become simpler and more intimate without being less solemn or realistic? Will it then suffice for us to point to the myriad liturgical *improvisations* that we have produced in recent years—with motives more theatrical than theological? What if the Romans teach the world that the essence of worship is man's faithful response to God's immediate and real presence in a community of men and women who love each other as they have been loved by God in Christ? Our only legitimate reaction would have to be a bold venture in basic liturgical reform ourselves.

Again, what would happen to us if—as now seems likely

—the final draft of the *Constitution on the Church* marks a giant forward step in Roman Catholic ecclesiology? We have debated the nature of the Church in denominational and ecumenical conferences for as long as I can remember —but the excellent things we have said have all too often been nullified by the actual effects of our sanctified divisions and our doctrinal confusions. Unless the Roman reactionaries succeed in scuttling the *Constitution on the Church,* both Protestants and Orthodox Christians will have to undertake a series of agonizing reappraisals of our "place" and our "mission" within the People of God. Why not?

In the course of the long debates in St. Peter's, I was repeatedly astonished (and here *my* biases kept breaking through!) to hear Catholic bishops talking earnestly about "the Word of God," "the People of God," "the priesthood of all believers," "the universal call to holiness" —phrases and notions that I could not classify otherwise than as "evangelical." Moreover, I kept running into obviously able men who are vividly alert to the issues involved —and more flexible in theological dialogue than the Orthodox theologians, or even many of my Protestant colleagues. I recall a lively discussion between Hans Küng and George Lindbeck, in which Küng claimed that *he* took Luther more seriously as a theologian than did Lindbeck —and Lindbeck was a Lutheran "observer"! But then Lindbeck takes St. Thomas more seriously than Küng seems to.

Thus, in random idle moments, I have wondered what would happen to Christianity if the Roman Catholic Church did, in fact, become at least minimally evangelical without becoming hopelessly divided in the process. It would change every conventional posture of every Christian communion in the world today.

Any such "danger" is still so slight that only the most fearful of us need be disturbed as yet. The council is no more than half over. The Roman traditionalists are by no means overwhelmed. Our non-Roman skeptics will continue to dampen the atmosphere. Even the Roman "moderates" are still deeply rooted in and committed to their partisan historic heritage—while the moderates on "our side" will soon enough turn wary if we ever come to really serious talk about *communicatio in sacris.*

God moves in mysterious ways his wonders to perform —this I know——but in none more mysterious, nor more ironic than in this curious turn of affairs that makes it at least barely possible that the most significant reform movement in the Christian community in the last half of the 20th century may be taking place in a tradition supposed to be unreformed and irreformable! Even if the final accounting on Vatican II is more modest than I both hope and expect it to be, it has already altered the basic terms in which Christians can henceforth consider the nature of the unity we seek. Thus, even those who have no interest whatsoever in immediate unity negotiations with Rome ought still to hope and pray that Vatican II *succeeds*—for all the "trouble" that would come upon us as the consequence of a revitalized Catholicism would surely be "a visitation from the Lord," a gauntlet and gage that we should rightly welcome!

CHAPTER 6

RELIGIOUS LIBERTY:
A PROTESTANT COMMENT

September 11, 1964

During session two, I had gotten acquainted with Father John Joyce, editor of *The Oklahoma Courier,* one of the livelier and more progressive of the several diocesan weeklies I had begun to read for background on Catholic reactions to the council. His invitation, in August, 1964, to write a "Protestant comment" on one of "the big issues before the council" was an unexpected but welcome opportunity to speak directly to grass-roots Catholics about the high stakes involved for us Protestants in the struggle over a conciliar affirmation of the basic human right to religious liberty.

Now that a declaration to this effect has been promulgated as an official council document, it may be too easily forgotten that, on the eve of session three, the whole issue was very much up in the air—and would remain so until the second week of session four! In session two, the immobilists had succeeded in detaching the chapter on religious liberty from its original locus in the *Decree on Ecumenism*—and in deferring a vote on the detached chapter. They would pursue this same strategy of deferment consistently to the bitter end. This meant that when I was writing this piece, the topic had no legal status on the council's agenda, its jurisdiction (under the Secretariat for Promoting Christian Unity) was still technically undetermined, and the Pope was under heavy pressure either to sidetrack the whole project or else to turn it over to the theological commission—which would have amounted to the same thing. The American bishops were solidly behind the declaration but many of their European brethren, although in favor of some such declaration, were quite dissatisfied with the form and argument of the original text.

The following "comment" was published in *The Oklahoma Courier* on September 11, just as I was leaving for Rome. More than once, during session three, I thought about it— especially during that grim closing week (November 17-22, 1964) when we saw a revised declaration deferred yet once more and the manifest will of the majority again frustrated. Since December 7, 1965, and the official *Declaration on Religious Liberty*, I have taken more satisfaction than I deserve from the fact that the core of my own argument for religious liberty in 1964 and that in the conciliar text of 1965 are obviously similar. Such things should be taken as ecumenical "signs of the times."

Every Roman Catholic must know by now that Vatican II has stirred great hopes and expectations among Protestants here and everywhere, and with good reason. In the past five years we have witnessed one marvel after another that would have been unthinkable a decade ago (e.g., the discoveries of Christian fellowship between Catholics and Protestants, the opening of new frontiers of ecumenical study and action). No man knows the full import of these developments, but many of us sincerely believe that they are truly providential.

At the same time, and naturally enough, there are lingering fears and doubts on both sides as to how far this new experiment in Catholic ecumenism can carry us toward that Christian unity for which we all ought to hope and pray. The serious ones among us are, rightly and reasonably, aware of the deep differences and the grave difficulties involved in any honest quest for unity. None of us wants it at the price of indifferentism or abjuration;

none of us should rest content with an amiable rearrangement of our inherited prejudices.

The council is faced with many momentous issues, and the greatest of these is the problem of the Church's *self*-understanding: the mystery of "the People of God," the manner of the Church's self-criticism. It is no accident that the *Constitution on the Church* has already been debated longer than any other schema before the council, or that it stands as the first item on the agenda of the upcoming third session, or that Pope Paul's first encyclical was entitled *Ecclesiam suam* (and is, rather obviously, his own "intervention" in the debate now coming up). Moreover, there are other great matters before the bishops besides ecclesiology proper (e.g., "episcopal collegiality," the relations between the episcopacy and the Roman curia, ecumenism, divine revelation, the Church in the modern world, etc.).

But, curiously enough, at least from the Protestant side, what may seem to Catholics as a "side issue" has come to stand as *the* crucial test case of the council's good faith in its total project. This is the *Declaration on Religious Liberty*. If Catholics are to comprehend the Protestant concern about this, they must try to understand the traditional Protestant fear of what we have taken to be the traditional Catholic equivocation at this point: namely, that Catholics believe themselves rightly entitled to a religious liberty which they would deny, on principle, to non-Catholics and unbelievers, if they could. Rightly or wrongly, we are still haunted by the ghost of Jan Hus at Constance—and, worse, by that council's maxim that "good faith need not be kept with heretics." We are still ravaged, spiritually, by the moral carnage of the Wars of Religion, of St. Bartholomew's Eve—and of religious persecutions in our own day. For its part, Rome has also had "a noble army of martyrs" down through the centuries—and none more heroic than in this very epoch! But is Rome prepared to affirm for others what it rightly claims for itself—and that not from expedience, but on principle and for conscience' sake? This question is not yet firmly settled—and it has come to be the touchstone by which all the other results of the council will be measured by us.

This is why, for example, we could so heartily second Archbishop Lucey's declaration in *America,* last spring: "The world is waiting for the Second Vatican Council to dispel once for all the suspicion that we preach two gospels of human rights according to circumstances." Noting that Pope John XXIII, in his great social encyclicals had called for "juridical guarantees of religious freedom (and all fundamental rights) under a system of constitutional government," the archbishop further declared, "It would be entirely appropriate that the American hierarchy should take the lead in the next session of the council to procure the adoption of a decree proclaiming authentic and universal freedom of religion, made permanent and unbreakable by constitutional guarantees."

This is also why, for us, one of the really tremendous climaxes of the council came last November 19, when Bishop E. J. M. De Smedt (of Bruges) delivered a great oration on the chapter on religious liberty—and was applauded to the rafters of St. Peter's by his brother bishops (and by us observers, too!). We were deeply moved by his strong, clear evocation of an older Catholicism than that of the Inquisition, by a doctrine of faith that challenged both Protestant individualism and Roman triumphalism in the same breath. As I sat there, gazing down the *aula*—jammed with 2,200 bishops—the thought flashed through my mind that if this council approves and promulgates *this* doctrine, it will force us Protestants into the ecumenical dialogue with Rome with weakened defenses and with heightened responsibilities. But, strangely enough, I found myself applauding this very prospect.

Bishop De Smedt clearly and firmly condemned "indifferentism" and "relativism"; he neither accepted nor condoned the existence of doctrinal error and religious unbelief in human society. What he did recognize, however, is that freedom is the mainspring of faith, whether of true faith or false. Religious faith is man's free response to God's free gift of grace. As such, it cannot be generated by force, nor can its opposite be suppressed by force. This means that religious faith and practice must have a broad range of real liberty, and this not only for the sake of the public good but also of the best interests of true religion. The only legitimate limitations of religious liberty have to do with culpable violations of other human rights and the disruption of public order. But this is a negative rule and cannot be invoked in support of religious coercion.

In situations where religious liberty obtains, men are free to persuade or to dissuade each other, to promote and practice their religion and to oppose contrary beliefs and practices. At the same time, such *propaganda fidei* must be conducted in a context of avowed respect for the human rights of dissenters, and with a genuine confidence that truth will win in a truly open forum. If anyone objects that this sounds more Protestant than Catholic, he has only to recall the famous declaration of Archbishop John B. Purcell of Cincinnati, making this same point nearly a hundred years ago—in the shadow of Vatican I:

> Our [American civil] constitution grants perfect liberty to every denomination of Christians . . . and I verily believe that this is infinitely better for the Catholic religion than were it the special object of the state's patronage and protection. All we want is a free field and no favor . . . truth is mighty and will prevail. . . . If men approve our religion, they will embrace it; if not they will stay away from it. I believe this is the best theory.[1]

[1] Cf. James J. Hennesey, *The First Vatican Council* (New York: Herder and Herder, 1963), p. 12.

Protestants have often spoken of the *right* of private judgment, in matters of conscience and belief—and we have all too often sounded as if we were contending for caprice. It would be truer to our own best heritage if we matched the *right* with the *duty* of "private" judgment. No man is exempt from authority in religion—and every man is obligated to square his internal authority with all legitimate external ones: Bible, Church, "right reason," duly constituted civil government, etc. But he cannot relegate to any of these, nor to all of them together, the aweful, God-given responsibility which is finally his alone: the choice of a posture of ultimate concern—even if it be the false postures of atheism or heresy. Men may be summoned and persuaded to faith; they may be guided in their expressions of faith; they may be governed in their religious practices—but they must not be coerced, *either way,* by any tyranny over mind or body. By now we know that coercion is an enemy of the truth, since it corrupts the very processes by which honest men are honestly convinced of the truth. "Error has no rights"—so runs the ancient slogan. But human beings have rights, and errors are not stifled when people are throttled. Heresy is not disposed of by faggots; truth is not served by bigotry.

It is my clear impression that if this issue comes to a vote in this forthcoming session, an affirmative declaration will be passed with a solid majority—led, as most observers agree, by the American hierarchy. But will it come to a vote? And if not, will it be further deferred, or even rejected? This, too, will depend largely on the American bishops. If they are really prepared to manifest their concern, the influence will be decisive and, I believe, affirmative. It may be truly providential that, out of the Catholic experience in the American experiment in church-state relations, there should come an authentic development of the ecumenical spirit implied in, and fostered by, an hon-

74

est commitment to religious liberty, in theory and practice. This will be an epochal contribution, not only to the Roman Catholic Church in the modern world but to all Christians, and not to Christians only but to all mankind!

CHAPTER 7

WILL THE DIEHARDS WIN?

December 28, 1964

The closing week of session three was widely regarded as a disaster by all the progressives—Catholics and Protestants alike. It began with the addition, under papal pressure, of a *nota praevia explicativa* to chapter three of the *Constitution on the Church* which beclouded the clear force of the doctrine of collegiality in the text. This was followed by a papal intervention that qualified the openness toward the Protestants in the draft of the *Decree on Ecumenism* already approved, penultimately, by the bishops. Further dismay came when the immobilist minority persuaded the presidency to defer a vote on religious liberty—and were upheld in this by the Pope. This series of victories allowed the immobilists by Paul VI was climaxed on the closing day when, in a plainly paraconciliar act, he added the phrase *Mater Ecclesiae* to the "Marian privileges," even though this same controverted phrase had been deliberately omitted from chapter eight of the *Constitution on the Church* by the (conservative) theological commission itself.

In the anguish and uproar that followed, the fear was voiced once more that the liberal cause might yet be lost and that the Pope had virtually thrown in with the diehards. I had scarcely got back home before Wayne H. Cowan, editor of the influential *Christianity and Crisis,* asked for an instant evaluation of the hue-and-cry. Under the circumstances, there was no time for reflection, but because the situation *was* critical—especially for the "public image" of Paul VI—I dashed off the following piece which appeared in the issue of December 28, 1964.

By now, it must be apparent that I was getting myself irretrievably committed to the progressive cause and to an optimistic view of its prospects in the council. It is a comfort not to have to imagine how embarrassing it would have been if that optimism had then been dashed by the council's outcome.

In the eyes of all "progressives" (including most of us in the observers' tribune) the third session of Vatican II was going extremely well until the very end—when many things seemed suddenly to go awry all at once. But our estimates of this "cloud at the close" have differed rather widely. Some saw it as evidence that the diehards still manned the portcullis of the apostolic palace; that they still hold the Pope in pawn; that they may finally succeed in their desperate efforts to restore the *status quo erat ante concilium.* Others of us agree, though rather ruefully, that in those closing days, the progressives lost a couple of conciliar battles but not the war, or anything close to it. This council is far too immense and cumulative an event to allow for final judgments, now or anytime soon. But this only means that those who realize that they, too, have a stake in it and its outcome must continue in their efforts to appraise the conciliar process as it unfolds and to ponder its puzzles for their meaning and portents. These comments are offered as a memorandum for such inquiries.

After a lumbering start in its opening week (September 14-18), session three began to move with gathering momentum and to register one progressive victory after another. There were positive victories on every issue (e.g., the votes on collegiality, ecumenism, religious liberty, the Church in the modern world, etc.). And there were negative victories, too (the remanding for drastic revision of several inadequate schemas, one of which [on missions] had been openly supported by Pope Paul himself). The famous "palace revolution" of October 8-13 was squelched with only minor damage—not, however, without wild outcries from liberals who seem still to fear that the immobilist minority really can, whenever they choose, snatch defeat from victory. This fear persists despite the public record which remains impressive: every issue that has been put to the council fathers for a vote, in all *three* sessions, has been carried by the progressive majority—unless you count the vote against young married deacons as a defeat (September 30, 1964). A note in my diary for October 2 reads:

> Another desultory debate. The majority of the speakers [on divine revelation] are *immobilisti,* but they seem clearly aware that the mind of the majority is set against them. Some seem resigned to defeat. Others sound as if they feel called upon to save the Church from the folly of this enchanted mob, by fair means or foul.

In early November, reports began to tell us of backstage delays in getting certain revised texts (the *Constitution on the Church,* chapter three [on collegiality], the *Decree on Ecumenism,* and the two declarations on religious liberty and the non-Christian religions) cleared for printing. The *Typis Polyglottis Vaticanis* is capable of producing a letter-perfect fascicle in less than 48 hours. Now, we heard, these controverted items were getting queued up in a traffic jam. This was the tip-off to impending trouble. Suspicions began to flare as our memories ran back to the parallel events of session two—the maneuvers that had side-tracked the earlier statements on religious liberty and on the Jews.

But the new texts finally appeared and were distributed —and a calendar of votes was set up for the congregations of November 17-21 to cover all of the separate sections. But then one noticed that the re-revised text of the *Declaration on Religious Liberty* was, in many important respects, a new document. It was, many of us thought, an even stronger statement than its predecessor, but I still recall my uneasy remembrance that article 30 of the *Ordo* stipulates that no *new* text shall be submitted to a vote without preliminary discussion. Naturally, the same thought occurred to others, on both sides. The progressives were satisfied that the spirit of the rule had been honored and were, therefore, disposed to "transcend" it. The diehards abominated any such text and were, therefore, prepared to invoke the rule to block it. With only three days left and a tight agenda, the moderators and presidents came up with a typical Roman compromise: let the fathers vote whether to vote on the declaration. This mild parliamentary irregularity opened the way for a swiftly organized power-play by the diehards. The next day, they presented a petition of conscience claiming that insufficient time had been allowed for the consideration of this new text and protesting that their rights under the *Ordo* had been infringed. It was an exciting morning— with most of the action taking place almost under my nose, directly before the observers' tribune. First there were Archbishops Dante and Staffa presenting the petition to Archbishop Felici (the general secretary); then its relay to Cardinal Tisserant (dean of the presidents); then a rapid sequence of consultations (with Cardinal Roberti, the council's parliamentarian, who naturally supported the *Ordo;* and with the moderators, who were visibly indisposed to go along). Meanwhile, Cardinal Tisserant was canvassing the other presidents until he had a majority (which meant that he left out Cardinal Meyer!). Then, finally, Tisserant's blunt and utterly self-assured an-

METHODIST OBSERVER AT VATICAN II

nouncement—there would be no vote on this text this session (and this followed by a flurry of widely scattered applause). The revolt that followed was wonderful to watch—with the towering figure of Cardinal Meyer over in the south transept, marshalling and deploying his troops as a general on the battlefield; and the gathering of more than 800 signatures to a petition to the Pope within the span of half an hour. It was convincing evidence that the progressive majority not only believed in collegiality but were determined to practice it. It was plain, however, that this progressive uprising had come too late and that it had been wrongly directed toward the Pope instead of the council presidents who were formally responsible for the decision. Given the rules and ethos of Vatican City, the Pope *had* to sustain his cardinal dean and the council parliamentarian. But the storm had two interesting sequels. When, the *next* morning (Friday), a similar move was made to defer action on the *Declaration on the Relationship of the Church to Non-Christian Religions*, both Archbishop Felici and Cardinal Tisserant recoiled from the petitioners in visible alarm. Moreover, the marked alteration of temper and resolution among the progressives was immediate and unconcealed. They had been had. They knew it, and they did not like it. And this is our best guarantee that, come session four, the opponents of religious liberty will have to risk an open vote on an issue that they rightly fear as fatal to their traditional triumphalism. Such a vote has been promised; this promise has now become a crucial test of the council's *bona fides*. The bishops intend to have it honored.

In this ruckus, as in others, it was instructive to watch the onset of the liberals' panic-syndrome and the cynics' vindication-complex. The first of these is somewhat similar to a manic-depression pattern, with mood-swings that range from soaring hopes of total victory to panic-fears of total defeat, with vivid bitterness toward the villains held responsible for so dire an insecurity. In the cynics' vindication-complex, one sees similar conclusions drawn from different premises. These are they—some of them Catholics, others Protestant (or Orthodox!), still others militant secularists—who have doubted from the start that leopards can change their spots or Romans abandon their triumphalism. Hence their welcome to any evidence which warrants an "I told you so." A recent editorial in *The Christian Century* illustrates this attitude with characteristic candor and miscomprehension:

> Before the council's third session began we predicted on the basis of our understanding of Pope Paul's encyclical *Ecclesiam Suam* that there is little hope for a permanent council in which the Pope and the bishops will share the rule of the Church. At times during recent weeks that prediction seemed rash. It no longer appears so. As we shall point out next week, the third session made some epochal decisions and pronouncements; but the monarchal [sic!] and hierarchal [sic!] structure of the Roman Catholic Church and the absolute supremacy of the Roman pontiff remain unchanged and undiminished. We have a council, but it is purely advisory.[1]

Neither perfectionism nor prejudice can provide us with a just perspective on Vatican II. There is no denying that if you measure its achievements, or even its brightest prospects, against the needs of the world or the hungers of men's hearts, it must be rated insufficient. But who can, by right, levy such a judgment? On the other side, if one *pre*-judges the council chiefly in terms of acrid memories, he is not likely to be either objective or fair. In this connection, it strikes me as ironic that many among us who have purged themselves (or at least their public utterances) of various sorts of their age-old ethnic prejudices toward Jews and Negroes, feel no such inhibitions about their anti-Catholic feelings.

[1] *The Christian Century*, LXXXI, No. 49 (December 2, 1964), p. 1483.

The one best hope I know for comprehending Vatican II lies in the rehearsal of its prehistory since the French Revolution and in a remembrance of the initial odds against its success when its first session was convened (October 11, 1962). When you begin to realize what has subsequently been achieved, in the face of an entrenched immobilism by an ill-organized and often inept coalition of progressives, Vatican II emerges as the start of a new chapter of modern church history. A major liturgical reform has already been started; a giant stride forward in ecclesiology has been taken; a new perspective in ecumenism has been framed; new vistas in Catholic self-understanding of the mission of the Church in the modern world have at least been opened up. The Roman Catholic episcopate has actually begun to be, and to act as, a *collegium episcoporum*. Finally (and this is fully as important as any of these other developments) the Roman Catholic intelligentsia (clerical *and* lay) have begun to breathe and think, and to speak up, in a new atmosphere of responsible freedom.

Even with its results thus far, Vatican II has achieved the minimal goals set for it by Pope John XXIII. In its two constitutions (on liturgy and on the Church) and its *Decree on Ecumenism*—not to speak of what we may yet hope for in session four—we have the first stage of a decisive mutation in the development of the Catholic tradition. In the tone and substance of the debates in St. Peter's, over three full sessions now, one can begin to recognize the genius of the conciliar process. Already there is a shift of gravitational fields in Roman Catholic polity—from a Mediterranean to a more truly global outreach; from centralized administration to a territorial pattern; from a triumphalist to a pilgrim Church. The *Roman* Catholic Church is beginning to be the Roman *Catholic* Church.

Can all this be nullified? Can the diehards win after all?

Let cynics believe this if they must, but then also know, quite clearly, that the evidence thus far available does not at all demand any such forebodings. It should, of course, go without saying that both the visionaries and the cynics will be dissatisfied with the outcome; that the council's consequences will be varied and confused; that the Roman Catholic Church has mounted a tiger, equally dangerous to ride or dismount from. It may also be expected that conservative reactions of various kinds will brake the surge of the progressive advance. It may very well be that Pope Paul himself will take the lead in balancing the polar tensions between papal primacy and episcopal collegiality. But the spirit of *aggiornamento* has been let loose in the world and it will not be readily suppressed.

The chief enigma in this complex and fluid situation is, of course, Pope Paul VI. It was perhaps inevitable that he should become the one last hope of the diehards and the prime suspect of the cynics. For both the bigots and the cynics seem to have agreed to discount the general drift of his published words and public deeds for the past 20 years. They are right, however, in realizing that as Pope one of his chief pastoral concerns is the unity and harmony of the strange mosaic that is the Roman Catholic Church. Session three laid bare the unbridged chasms of thought and feeling that divide the diverse tendencies in the council; it forced showdowns on thorny issues that had hitherto been moot. Moreover, it must be admitted that the diehard minority was largely ignored—until they struck back with the only weapons they had left.

Paul VI is a veteran of the Roman curia, heir of Vatican I, and successor to the last four Piuses, as well as John XXIII. Those who speak of him as weak or indecisive happen to be those who also have demanded of him partisan judgments of partisan issues—and who are impatient with his manifest intention to serve as both the agent and symbol of the Church's *unity*. Thus, they find it easy to

83

misconstrue his frequent references to the Petrine Office (as in *Ecclesiam Suam* and in several "public audiences" during session three). But with collegiality now getting its belated due, who is there to uphold the organic unity of papacy *and* episcopacy? Certainly not the immobilist opponents of collegiality; and, just as certainly, not those who brush aside the immense residual difficulties in the interpretation of the new doctrine as now proclaimed.

It goes far beyond the evidence, therefore, to say that Pope Paul disbelieves the doctrine of collegiality or that he aims to nullify it. One might, however, wonder if he has, as yet, understood or fully accepted what the doctrine implies in practice. This question was raised, rather starkly, by his puzzling paraconciliar actions in those anti-climactic days at the end of the session. On Tuesday, November 17, he submitted to Cardinal Bea and Bishop Willebrands (of the Secretariat for Promoting Christian Unity) a list of amendments to the text of the *Decree on Ecumenism*—then scheduled for its final vote in congregation on Friday. Only two of the changes were materially significant (both dealing with passages in that remarkable second half of chapter three, which describes the Protestant "Churches and ecclesial communities in the West" in terms more sympathetic and generous than any Protestant description of Roman Catholicism I have ever seen) and what they do is to bring the text more closely into line with the actuality of general Catholic feeling. What *was* alarming about this papal intervention was its timing and manner—this by a man who is noted for his sense of timing and protocol. Bea and Willebrands had to accept or reject the amendments without being able to consult their Secretariat; and the price of rejection was, of course, postponement—an anti-climax, indeed! Why had the Pope waited so long (the text had, presumably, been on his desk for three weeks) and why was his intervention so awkward? Thus far, I've found no convincing answer to this dual question—despite the flood of comment on it.

Even stranger, I thought, was his seizing the occasion of the closing public session (November 22) to make his declaration that the Blessed Virgin Mary is *Mater Ecclesiae*—this in addition to the catena of reverential titles already strung out in chapter eight of the *Constitution on the Church,* which he had promulgated 30 minutes earlier. Here again, the crucial point was not doctrinal. One need not doubt that the Pope believes in *Maria Mater Ecclesiae,* or that he has the right to teach it. But why in this particular setting—in the face of the assembled college of bishops in a solemn public session with no prior consultation, and after the theological commission (notoriously conservative) had already decided, by vote, to omit this particular Marian "privilege"? What may be a partial answer struck me as I looked across the *aula* and saw there, in the *periti's* tribune, Monsignor Carlo Balic (consultor to the Holy Office and ardent in his Marian zeal) shouting for joy and embracing his colleagues. It crossed my irreverent mind that the Pope had gone out of his way to give these people a small triumph to celebrate on their tumbril's journey into yesterday.

Even so, the really hard questions persisted. Was this a *deliberate* manifestation of "the Pope above the council"? Was this a fair sample of Paul's *basic* understanding of the Petrine Office? Was this the price a Pope who abhors schism is willing to pay for the support of the diehards (there were only five *non-placets* on the final vote)? Is it possible that Pope Paul is now *caput* of an episcopal college which is further along than he in its willingness to commit the Church to the risks of reform and ecumenical dialogue? I do not have good answers to these questions; we may have to wait for such answers until much more evidence is in. But before we join the chorus of Paul's dispraisers, we ought to recollect his role in dismantling the conservative opposition and in swelling the progressive majorities in session three over those in session two. Between these two sessions there was a shift of at least 200 votes from the conservative to the progressive side of the balance. The only intelligible explanation I can offer for this is that they were directly assured by the Pope himself that *he* was confident of the future of an "open Church." This, as much as any other single factor, has sealed the fate of the *immobilisti*.

They can, and will, continue their obstructionist tactics, but they have lost their initial control of the council. They can, and will, continue to enlist the Pope's sympathies and sentiments but, in the end, this will not amount to a veto upon conciliar decisions. Over against this, it seems equally clear—and this goes with his character and style—that Pope Paul does not intend for the diehards to be humiliated in their defeat. He is willing, even eager, to mollify their frustrations as these mount up in the council's forward motion. For, remember, he is leading a reformation *Roman-style*—and the rest of us will have to muster what tolerance and patience we can in order to appreciate and respond to its distinctive ambivalences. It would help if in doing so we temper our natural self-righteousness with the sobering thought that none of us can point to any recent experiments in reform and renewal in our traditions that can match what's been happening in Rome.

The "success" of Vatican II will more nearly pose than solve the real issues of what Pope Paul speaks of as "the recomposition of Christian unity." What it will do is to provide Roman Catholics with a full generation's efforts at assimilation and development—and non-Romans with at least as much. What matters, *ad interim,* for them and for us, is that we take on as a crucial enterprise for the Christian future, the continuing effort to understand the council in its fullest possible depth—its baffling prehistory, its ponderous processes, its curious anomalies and confusions, its inexplicable stability, its undeniable charisms, its unpredictable consequences. Otherwise, we may readily miscalculate the direction and force of its multiple impacts in the Christian community and in the modern world—and so, even with goodwill, misjudge our own responsibilities in the manifest *kairos* of these times.

CHAPTER 8

THE COUNCIL AT MIDPOINT

February 2, 1965

One of the intended functions of the delegated-observers was to relay their impressions of the council back to their respective constituencies. I attempted to do this in many different ways: written reports to the World Methodist Council, oral reports to our General Conference Commission on Ecumenical Affairs, news stories in denominational papers, addresses to church gatherings of various sorts and sizes. One of the most important of these opportunities for interpreting the council came on February 2, 1965, at a convocation of some 1,200 Methodist ministers from seven south central states at Southern Methodist University. These men were interested in ecumenism and they are influential opinion makers in the Protestant Churches in the region.

By February 2, the cloud at the close of the council had largely dissipated—and the wave of criticism had begun to wash back out again. The Pope's visit to India, his appointment of a batch of new cardinals and, above all, the announcement of the opening date and the initial agenda for session four had brightened its prospects considerably. The skeptics, however, were still pounding away, and on the other side, the Catholic traditionalists (e.g., Father De Pauw and Evelyn Waugh) had begun to grumble out loud about "the Protestantizing tendencies" of the council, with a particular grievance against the change from their cherished all-Latin masses. Even though there was only one more session scheduled, 11 of the 16 schemas on the docket were still in various stages of development. The council really was, therefore, at a "midpoint"—and, in my report to my fellow ministers, it was my chief concern to help them understand the background, the dynamics and the prospect of the conciliar process.

Here we are, ten weeks after the close of Act III of Vatican II and seven months away from the rising of the curtain on Act IV—presumably the finale. It has been scheduled to open on September 14, and no date has been set for its *adjournment!* Meanwhile, however, we have had an announcement from Rome as to the initial agenda for the session, and now, last week, the Pope's appointment of 27 new cardinals—a highly important barometer reading for the weather picture ahead. We are all aware that the council has stirred the imaginations of all sorts and conditions of men throughout the world with its promise of significant change in the oldest and, we had supposed, the most tradition-ridden of all ecclesiastical institutions.

Routine news is boring, bad news is fascinating, but good news has its own especial excitement if it really is *good* news. And the hope has been raised, and spread abroad, that Vatican II really *is* good news—not only for the Roman Catholic Church but for Christendom and the world. The prospect of a reformation, or renovation, in the Roman Catholic Church is either exhilarating or alarming, depending on your hopes and fears. This is at least one reason why you can get so many different—and contradictory—appraisals of Vatican II, ranging from naive to cynical. Already the council has achieved more than had ever been predicted by the most optimistic progressives five years ago. And yet, every setback to the cause of reform still raises the cry among the bigots that all this talk of reform is a smoke screen for a typically Roman plot to weaken our resistance to their monopolistic schemes. The current issue of a well-known anti-Catholic periodical expresses, in its own hysterical rhetoric, an attitude I've encountered elsewhere both in America and in Europe:

> The collapse and failure of the third session of the Vatican Council has left us at POAU headquarters with feelings of disappointment and disgust.
>
> The disappointment lies in the fact that this important body should have failed so abjectly in regard to religious liberty and, instead of moving in the direction of reform, actually solidified the totalitarian rule of the Pope over the Roman Catholic Church.
>
> The disgust is with ourselves—that we should have entertained and expressed real hope for the Vatican Council. We, of all people, should have known better. We believe now that, since the death of Pope John, the thing has been hopeless.
>
> One thing can and should be done: blame should be fairly placed. This is not difficult to do. The blame for the failure lies squarely on the shoulders of a reactionary Pope—Paul VI. Under his leadership Vatican II exposed the Roman Church as the same old feudal operation run by the same old dictator under the same old claim that he is God's regent on earth. When Pope John died the council died. Pope Paul VI has identified himself as a man of firm 16th-century mentality, a junior model of Pius XII—less intelligent, less able, less adroit—but more tyrannical.[1]

There is at least one error in every sentence of this outburst—and they vary from misunderstanding to slander—but it illustrates very well the sort of Protestant bigotry that matches, snarl for snarl, the rabid temper of the reactionaries in Rome. But when we compare something like this with many other varying judgments from more competent observers, we begin to realize just how difficult

[1] *Church and State*, Vol. 18, No. 1 (January, 1965), p. 11.

it is to get Vatican II into a just perspective and to understand the news that flows from it like a flood.

It goes without saying that I do not suppose that I really understand this incredibly complex operation. But after five years of trying, I do think I've come up with a sort of general formula as to the necessary prerequisites for interpreting this epoch-making event in the church history of our lifetime. The formula has been tested and confirmed on the spot in Rome and also here at home, where all I have is what anyone else may have, plus a trickle of correspondence and documentation from my friends in Rome. Without some sort of perspective like this (or its equivalent) it is altogether too easy, even for interested people, to miss the really critical points in this news report or that document—or else to misconstrue them.

To begin with there is the tangled prehistory of the council, running back to the Reformation and even before that—but focused chiefly in the last 200 years in the bitter struggles between the Roman Church and the Enlightenment, between the papacy and the secular governments of Europe. It began when the Bourbons and the Hapsburgs forced Clement XIV to suppress the Jesuits in 1773, chiefly because of their support of papal supremacy. It continued with the persecution of the Church by the French revolutionaries and the humiliations of Pius VI by Joseph II of Austria and by Napoleon—and the five-year imprisonment of Pius VII by Napoleon. Then came the tragic struggle over the political unification of Italy (1848-70) and the militant reaction of Pio Nono against secular liberalism and all its works. In the course of this conflict came the dogma of the Immaculate Conception (1854), the *Syllabus of Errors* (1864) and Vatican I (1869-70)— which is best understood as the bishops rallying around the beleaguered Pope and confirming both his supremacy and infallibility. Thus was established the spirit of *piononismo,* which continued dominant in Rome, with minor modifications, until the death of Pope Pius XII in 1958—the spirit of outright rejection of the Enlightenment world-view; the point-blank refusal to accept the disestablishment of the Church as a sovereign temporal power; the monopoly of scholasticism in Roman universities and seminaries; the two Marian dogmas; the condemnation of modernism; the rejection of the ecumenical movement; the entrenchment of the Roman curia; the heyday of Roman triumphalism, etc., etc. What all of this did was to turn the Roman Church into a citadel under siege—well-manned, self-sufficient and surprisingly effective in its mission in some parts of the world (notably America)—but still on the defensive and hurting from her losses to the Communists and to the secularists.

This was Rome's posture when Pope John XXIII called the bishops into council. This explains how the old Romans felt—and still do—about the bare notion of *aggiornamento*. This is why Vatican II is so profoundly disturbing to many Catholic faithful who actually liked it the way it was in their old ghettoes. Moreover, this prehistory hasn't been forgotten—the memories and residues of two centuries have not been washed away. One runs into them in Rome, as vivid still as yesterday. It is always against *this* background that you have to interpret every proposal and speech in St. Peter's, every document (almost every phrase in some documents), every action of every commission, every word and gesture of the Pope. When you consider the inherently conservative character of religious institutions—however radical their pronouncements—you can only wonder at the magnitude of what is being dreamed and proposed and *partially achieved* in Vatican II.

In the second place, it is necessary to realize in advance what they are *trying to do* in this council—and what they are *not* trying to do—in order to measure their achievements and failures with any accuracy at all. It is, one must remember, chiefly a domestic affair of the Roman Catholic Church—despite the fact that they have opened it to observers and journalists and the eyes of the world. The fathers of the council are trying to decide what is wise and good for the Roman Catholic Church, and only indirectly what will meet the demands of the Eastern Orthodox, the Protestants, the Jews, the journalists—and the POAU! This is why they spend more time on intramural questions than we outsiders readily appreciate. Another way of saying the same thing is that Vatican II is an experiment in renewing the Roman Catholic Church for its own mission in the world—which it considers as an indirect preparation for church unity negotiations with its separated Christian brethren, if and when. Rome is not now formulating its terms for "the recomposition of Christian unity." Rather, it is trying to put its own house in order and to put the rest of Christendom on notice that union, if it is ever to be considered, will also demand equivalent renewals on their part. To this end, they have laid out an agenda that revolves around two poles: ecclesiological self-understanding and ecclesiastical retooling. The two most fundamental documents of the council (the *Constitution on the Sacred Liturgy* and the *Constitution on the Church*) have already been promulgated; they are open for public study and are already beginning to be implemented at parish and diocesan levels. Everything else on the agenda of the council is either an "enabling act" or a practical application of the principles of vital worship or the bishops' basic understanding of the nature of the Church.

For us, the *Decree on Ecumenism* is the point that matters most; for them, it is a corollary of the *Constitution on the Church*. For us, the declarations on religious liberty and the non-Christians are tests of the good faith of the council as a whole—and the progressive majority in the council understands this and agrees with it. But in the deepest logic of the council these things are consequences or presuppositions of the really fundamental developments in liturgy, episcopal collegiality and the apostolate of the laity. This holds as well for the schema on the Church in the modern world and that cluster of propositions about missions, monasticism, Christian education, marriage, etc., etc.

In the third place, it is necessary to distinguish in advance between the *drama* of the council and the *process* of the council. The drama consists in the fuss and feathers, the clashes between the good guys and the bad guys, in the rejection of that awful text on the two sources of revelation (October 20, 1962), the straw votes on collegiality (October 30, 1963), that wild Thursday morning (November 20, 1964) when the *Declaration on Religious Liberty* got derailed and the progressives rose up in belated and unavailing revolt, the Pope's paraconciliar interventions in the closing days of the session—and now his appointment of 27 new cardinals. The *process* of the council consists in the incredibly arduous work of the conciliar commissions, of the scholars and journalists, in Rome and elsewhere; and, above all, in the massive enterprise of the re-education of 2,500 Roman Catholic bishops in the issues and options with which they are being confronted. This is a hopelessly complex process but it helps to realize that it proceeds in two separate but interacting rhythms: the rhythm of *discussion* and the rhythm of *decision*.

The rhythm of discussion includes the drafting and the sifting of a mountain of documents and commentaries, in the debates in the commissions, in the informal discussions in the coffee bars and elsewhere, in the informal caucuses and backstage maneuverings—in the ebb and flow of gossip which forms so vital a part of the Roman way of life. More formally, it is manifest in the 1,800 ten-minute speeches that have been delivered in the three sessions, by men from all over the geographical and ideological maps—and there are samples from everywhere and of all sorts. The mentality of the bishops in the *aula* ranges from pre-Copernican to post-Einstein, from the mustiest old orthodoxy to the rawest "new theology"—with a sprinkling of heresy now and then for seasoning. There was, for example, the bishop who declared feelingly that the religion closest to Christianity was *not* Judaism or Islam—as the others had argued—but *animism!* As long as issues are in the rhythm of discussion, they are up for grabs—and the utmost freedom is allowed and exercised in the expression of various views and positions. For example, there was the day when our own Bishop Martin happened to be visiting (October 29). Archbishop Dearden, the *relator* for the report on the Christian family, specifically requested the fathers not to debate it publicly at this time—because the crucial question of birth control had been reserved by the Pope for future determination. Whereupon—boom!—Cardinals Léger and Suenens and the Patriarch Maximos blew the lid off by directly expounding the theological and ethical issues involved in the question of conjugal love. Or again, there was the day when Pope Paul came into the council and encouraged the bishops to accept the schema on the missionary activity of the Church. He was scarcely out of the *aula* before the critics fell upon the schema tooth and nail—and the bishops sent it back to its commission for a thorough overhaul.

The other main dimension of the conciliar process—the rhythm of *decision*—proceeds at three levels. First, after a schema has been debated, there is a preliminary vote as to whether it is good enough to bother with thereafter. These preliminary votes are *placet* (yes) or *non-placet* (no). Then, after further discussion *in specie* (section by section), there are intermediate votes that allow for amendments and revisions of the texts. These may be yes, no, or *placet iuxta modum* (yes, with qualifications)—and the amendment must be submitted in writing to the secretary general along with the *placet iuxta modum*. These amendments are then considered and incorporated into the revised text by the appropriate commission and brought back to the council for review. If the bishops are satisfied with what the commissions have done with their amendments, the way is then cleared for the final vote which, like the preliminary ones, are yes or no. It is worth noting that in the course of the discussion opinions will vary widely—even wildly. In the decisions there has been a steadily rising fraction of progressive unanimity ranging from 80 percent at the lowest to better than 99 at the highest. On one vote, there were 11 negatives cast against the proposition that bishops and priests should cooperate in their ministry to the faithful. And, on another, 49 bishops voted against a literal quotation from the dogma of papal supremacy and infallibility from Vatican I.

A fourth prerequisite understanding, if you are to read the news from Vatican II intelligently, is the realization that this is a "Reformation Roman-Style"—and so, unlike anything *we* are accustomed to (or that *they* have been for so long as makes no matter). Such a reform is based on the premise that no "development" can be allowed that repudiates any of Rome's fundamental positions—doctrinal, canonical, hierarchical. *Semper idem!* It is to this rock of ages that the *immobilisti* cling; it is to the continuity and validity of historic tradition that they appeal. The problem, of course, is what is really *fundamental* and what is capable of "development." In Christian history generally, reform and radical change have usually been accompanied by schisms and separations. This is why Catholic Christianity fears radical change—why there is such a genuine horror of innovation in the very depths of the Catholic mentality.

And yet Vatican II is changing, not the substance of Catholic teaching, but its mode and manner and spirit. For their rationalization of this spirit of change-without-discontinuity, Vatican II has turned for its most distinctive theme to the doctrine of *development*—the idea, so deeply probed by John Henry Cardinal Newman, that progress is possible without the annulment of traditions, that valid progress may grow out of the living past without rupture, that the only sort of progress that is really viable is that which is rooted in vital tradition.

If you will analyze the actions of Vatican II in this light, you can more fully appreciate their magnitude and import. Take for example the reform of the liturgy promulgated last year in the *Constitution on the Sacred Liturgy*. Here we have liturgical traditions which had been fixed for 400 years *developed* in terms of liturgical principles drawn from an older and more truly catholic tradition of sacramental theology and liturgical practice. But, practically and psychologically speaking, this "development" is a very real change to the vast majority of Catholic priests and laymen—and for some it amounts to a painful rupture with the past.

Or again, take this complicated business of "collegiality," and its relation to papal primacy as defined in Vatican I. The *immobilisti* have fought this on the grounds that episcopal collegiality reduces papal primacy in theory and will diminish it in practice. No progressive will admit this; none could afford to. Hence, *they* argue that collegiality will actually develop the significance of the Petrine Office—though they do admit, with some relish, that collegiality in practice will weaken the traditional control of the Roman curia over the Petrine Office. The gist of the doctrine of collegiality is that the pope and all the other bishops share in the government of the Church as successors to the college of the apostles, with the pope as Peter's successor, the constitutional head of the college. Now, in the penultimate text of this chapter—the last before it was finally published for promulgation—there was a *nota explicativa* (an explanatory note) that is a veritable marvel of theoretical ingenuity, the nerve of which is that collegiality does not set up a second center of authority and unity over the pope. One of my friends (an American bishop) told me about asking Cardinals Ottaviani and Doepfner their respective opinions of this *nota*. Ottaviani was delighted: "It's excellent; it means that we can accept the chapter." Doepfner was resigned: "It's all right: because it's the *text* that counts after all." The obvious moral to this story is that the real meaning of collegiality has still to be worked out empirically by what the bishops and the pope *do together* in their actual practice of shared leadership and responsibility—and it will take a generation before this eventuality will be determined.

The *Constitution on the Church* is the most basic of all the documents of Vatican II. It is an extraordinary exercise in self-examination and self-commitment in the light of divine revelation and historical responsibility. It describes the Church both as it is (empirically) and as it ought to be (imperatively)—and then challenges all Catholics to understand themselves as members of the Church so conceived. Even in its bare outline one can see how this constitution rests on tradition and yet reaches out toward new frontiers: 1. the Church as the mystery wrought by God in gathering his children into a saving community of faith and grace; 2. the Church as the pilgrim People of God, on the move in the present and open to the future, with definite goals of pilgrimage in this world and the next; 3. the principle of corporate or shared leadership in the universal Church as a crucial element in the very notion of catholicity; 4. the general apostolate, or priesthood, of *all* members of the Church; hence a vital role for the laity in Christian evangelism and witness, in Christian education and in Christian service; 5. the universal call to holiness which is declared to be an imperative for every Christian in whatever station or duty in life; 6. the special vocations of monastic dedication and service; 7. the pilgrim Church on earth in relation to the Church triumphant in heaven; 8. the Blessed Virgin Mary, as the first and principal member of the Church and hence a model of the meaning of church membership. Even in this last chapter—so difficult for Protestants (and made no easier at all by Pope Paul's arbitrary addition of *Maria Mater Ecclesiae* to the text)—we still have an interesting example of progressive change. The *original* proposal (which had very strong—indeed highly emotional—support) was to devote an entirely separate schema to Mary, which would have undoubtedly gone very much farther in Marian devotion than this present chapter of the *Constitution on the Church,* or even the Pope's contribution.

If you take seriously this background I have sketched in —and particularly this notion of "Reformation Roman-Style"—you then can read with real appreciation the now official *Decree on Ecumenism.* Everyone knows that the traditional position of the Roman Catholic Church for 400 years has been rigidly self-contained; that for 50 years now they have held aloof from the so-called ecumenical movement among Protestants, Anglicans and Orthodox Christians. Yet in the conciliar *Decree on Ecumenism* we now have an unprecedentedly open and generous statement of (1) Catholic principles of ecumenism; (2) guidelines for the practice of these principles by Roman Catholics— including suggestions for common ecumenical services of prayer and a look down the way toward more intimate relationships of membership and ministry and an eventual *communicatio in sacris;* (3) how the Orthodox and Protestant Churches are to be viewed through Roman Catholic eyes. This last section is quite remarkable—I know nothing to match it, certainly not in the literature of our denomination, nor in the literature of the World Council of Churches.

Some of you will undoubtedly expect a comment on the hullabaloo about religious liberty and the Pope's interventions in the last week of session three, but I have already been over this in two or three speeches which some of you have heard and in two different articles which some of you may have read and I've no inclination to rerun *that* tape just now.[2] The gist of the matter was this: the bishops did not receive the revised draft of the *Declaration on Religious Liberty* until Monday morning of the final week—with a Saturday adjournment staring them in the face. The major blame for this delay belongs to the stalling tactics of the diehards who utterly abhor this whole project and rightly fear that it will mean the end of *their* world. But *some* of the responsibility lay with the Secretariat for Promoting Christian Unity which had prepared the revision. They did not drop their *textus re-emendatus* into the council hopper until the first of November—and it *was* a new text. It was on this point that the diehards pounced and here they were technically right, for article 30 of the *Ordo* of the council specifies that no vote is to be taken on a schema in particular until it has been freely debated in general. The diehards appealed to this article and claimed that their freedom in council had been abrogated by the demand that they vote without adequate time for study. On this point Tisserant (the dean of the council presidency) backed them up, Roberti (the council parliamentarian) backed him up—and then the Pope had to back them both up.

In the ensuing uproar, religious liberty has now become a *cause célèbre*—not only in the council and in the Catholic world but throughout the Christian community, and beyond. This means that there is bound to be a vigorous ferment of discussion between now and session four, and some fairly careful planning to insure a decisive vote. In my judgment, it is actually better to do it this way, because now, when the decision does come, we shall have an even clearer and firmer statement of religious liberty—and it

[2] See below, pp. 121-138, 146-152.

will be all the more secure because it will have been achieved in an open forum, in the teeth of desperate but futile opposition.

And now we have Act IV coming up. Already the noises of the scene-shifters are more than faintly audible backstage. The first thing to count on is the unexpected. This comes partly from the Roman love of secrecy and surprise; it comes also from their deep-grained habit of improvisation—of reacting swiftly to some new opening or turn of events. Although it seems a very cumbersome operation, the Vatican (and now the council) can shift directions or switch plans more nimbly than any other outfit I have ever seen in action. The results are often surprising to outsiders (and sometimes to the insiders as well).

For example, when I left Rome in late November, there was widespread in very high quarters the talk that the Pope would make no new cardinals until the end of the council—and even might let the college dwindle back to its original status as the administrative staff of the diocese of Rome. Now, suddenly, we have 27 new ones—and nobody I know has been told if this was simply a well-kept secret (which seems implausible to me) or an extemporary move by Pope Paul to write some more handwriting on the wall for the fathers of the council to decipher. Moreover, the list requires some deciphering: not a single *prominent* immobilist (unless you count Archbishop Dante) and yet also none of the fair-haired boys from among the zealots. All but six or seven of them are "moderate" to "progressive" and the whole group has an obvious international flavor—so that now the bloc of curial cardinals is outgunned and outmanned.

But not all is concealed either. The initial agenda for session four has been set—with all the hot items queued up for the opening fireworks: religious liberty, the Church in the modern world, the missionary activity of the

Church, and the non-Christian religions. Thus the Pope's promise for action on religious liberty has been honored this much; the progressives will see to it that the rest of the promise will also be honored. The declaration *will* be voted on. And when they vote, my guess is that there will be fewer than 175 *non-placets* in the preliminary vote,[3] less than 300 amendments in the intermediate vote;[4] and less than 75 *non-placets* on the final vote[5]—even though this will be the most drastic single break with Catholic tradition of any council action. If they reject this declaration and fail to pass another which is reasonably straightforward and unambiguous, I'll eat my crow unsalted and ruefully apply for membership in the POAU.

Meanwhile, however, it will be interesting and important for you to watch the Catholic press and to talk with your Catholic neighbors and friends about the impact of the council on the ordinary life and experience of Catholic Christians. In so doing, though, you must keep reminding yourself that the entire American Catholic Church up until just 50 years ago was a missionary operation of the *Propaganda Fidei* and has had a "settled" *national* hierarchy for scarcely a full generation. This means that what is now happening to American Catholics—what with vernacular masses and marriages, what with Catholic-Protestant gatherings of various sorts breaking out all over, what with the debate about "the pill" and the rash of unfamiliar theological notions popping up in their papers and pulpits, etc.—all this is much more drastic than any ecclesiastical change that has ever happened to any of us or, alas, is likely to. No wonder, then, that many of the Catholics are suffering from "*aggiornamento* jitters"—that many are bewildered and confused. The real wonder and promise of

---

[3] The decisive vote came on September 21; the *non-placets* numbered 224.
[4] There were 373.
[5] There were 70—who were promptly dubbed "the Septuagint."

it all, however, comes from the astonishingly positive reactions of the articulate majority—not only of the Catholic intellectuals, but also from the rank and file.

And now, what about *us*? What about *our* role and responsibility in this new "epoch of Vatican II"? In what ways shall we respond to the initiative the Catholics have set in motion and how shall we react to the new opportunities for Christian cooperation which are opening up before us?

In the closing section of *Ecclesiam Suam*, Pope Paul has sketched out the main lines of his answer to this problem in terms of a multi-level "dialogue." This basic idea of *dialogue as an act of love toward other Christians* was echoed time and time again in St. Peter's and in the commission meetings. It is essentially the spirit that prompts us to recognize our separated brethren, Catholic or Protestant, as *brethren in Christ*. It is the spirit of listening, of learning, of trying to understand another's history and heritage. It is the search for unity in the belief that Christian unity lies ahead of us and not in a return to some vanished golden age.

Thus the first great challenge of Vatican II is to new experiments in dialogue, so conceived, and to new adventures in Christian acquaintance and cooperation. The council has challenged us all to learn about each other and to appreciate more positively the great treasures of Christian tradition and fidelity in other Churches and communities about which so many of us know so little. We are challenged to be self-critical, to consider those aspects and elements in our own lives and traditions that are inauthentic, that need reform, renewal and rededication to the service of God in Christ. We are challenged to rethink the missionary task of the Church, of the ministries of the Word and Sacraments in the development of a truly humane culture, and of a fit society for God's children to grow up in. One of the greatest of all the consequences of Vatican

II for the Catholics of the world has been to stir them out of their "dogmatic slumbers" and to turn them to face the modern world as they have not for 200 years—to risk their future in aggressive, dynamic evangelism rather than in defensive self-preservation.

But, really, the very same challenge lies at the door of *all* Christians, and this is the main reason why all of us who bear the Christian name are under the imperative to seek for Christian unity and to exploit the unity we already have, not only with our lips but in our lives. As a consequence of Vatican II, the Roman Catholic Church is committed to major new developments in almost every dimension of her life and work. They are making an heroic effort now to transcend their past without repudiating that past. They are attempting a reform in continuity with their longer, richer traditions of catholicity. But change *is* happening all the same, and these changes will be felt throughout the Catholic Church, throughout the Christian community, throughout the world.

Moreover, the ecclesiastical situation has been changed for Protestants and Orthodox Christians, too, whether or not we are pleased with the changes or eager to respond to them affirmatively. The old patterns of Catholic-non-Catholic relations will change at an accelerated rate. Non-Catholics will have to react one way or another to "the new Church" that is being formed in the Christian community by the renewal of the Roman Catholic Church through Vatican II. One thing is sure: in the aftermath of this council, all Christians will have to take the Roman Catholic Church far more seriously into account than we have done in the last century or so. Even in opposition or competition, we will have to reckon with them in terms that are quite different from those supplied by our conventional stereotypes.

What we might hope and pray for is that along with the renewal in the Roman Catholic communion, there may also come renewals of life and power in our own Protestant communities—to the end that, renewed in the inner springs of our Christian life and in the outward expressions of our Christian obedience, we may go forward together toward that unity which Christ wills for his Church, in those ways in which we may be led by God's good providence—*if* we are truly open to *his* Spirit and truly obedient to *his* will.

CHAPTER 9

THE DOCTRINE OF THE LAITY

April 29, 1965

In March, 1965, I was at the Southern Baptist Theological Seminary in Louisville, Kentucky, doing the Norton Lectures, when I got a call from Martin Work, executive director of the National Council of Catholic Men, inviting me to address the biennial convention of the NCCM meeting in Dallas the following month. It was an awkward assignment to add to an already staggering schedule, but there were two commanding reasons for undertaking it. One was that this was another "first" in the Catholic-Protestant dialogue—for the NCCM and for me. The second was my conviction that the new developments in the doctrine of the laity constituted one of the council's most significant achievements—both for church renewal and also in ecumenical outreach.

At the time of the convention (April 29) the interim affairs of the council were in something of a lull. There was, of course, the continuing agitation against religious liberty and, besides, the Pope was under heavy pressures from many quarters in the matter of a proposed declaration on Catholic-Jewish relations. The *Decree on the Apostolate of the Laity* was still very much in process—so that all I had to go on, in terms of official documentation, was chapter four of the *Constitution on the Church*. But that was enough, for I had come to regard that particular chapter as one of the most remarkable passages in the whole of the conciliar literature, both in its doctrinal perspective and in its practical import. It was this perspective and its implications that I wanted to stress to the lay delegates in the convention, and to their clerical colleagues as well.

It was an unusual sequel to my speech to the bishops in Rome—for here, in my own home town, I was talking to the representatives of the Catholic laity from all over America. Their interest and response was yet another testimony to the fact that "the epoch of Vatican II" had fully dawned even before the council was concluded.

It is, of course, something of an innovation for a Protestant theologian to be here on this occasion—and my first word must be one of the lively appreciation for the great honor and opportunity it involves. One of the nicest things about it all is how much "at home" I feel among you and in the reverend presence of two of my favorite bishops, Bishop Gorman and Bishop Leven. The fact is that my experiences as a delegated-observer at Vatican II have greatly enlarged and enriched my contacts with Catholics, both clergy and lay, both in Rome and here in America. Indeed, they have given me something of a temporary VIP status—undeserved, of course, but heartily enjoyed nonetheless. Over the past four years I have developed a quite positive sense of identification with *your* council, and I find myself, as often as not, speaking of *our* council: what *we* have already accomplished, what *we* still have to do, etc.

For the plainest fact about Vatican II is that it has come to stand as a landmark in modern church history— an historic turning point between an old era whose passing we need not mourn and a new epoch of renewal and advance, the full import of which we cannot yet see. You know even better than I how much interest it has generated—and how much confusion, too; confusion that has been aptly tagged, "*aggiornamento* jitters." Already in its *Constitution on the Sacred Liturgy, Constitution on the Church,* and *Decree on Ecumenism,* this council has opened up an immense frontier for development and progress, not only within your own communion but in Christendom as a whole and in the world as well.

The chief justification for my presuming to talk to you today springs from my enthusiasm for what Vatican II is trying to do. I am here as a spokesman for that myriad of non-Catholic Christians who are "rooting" for the council's success and who believe that if you succeed, even partially, with the renovation of the Church already begun, the consequences will be immensely beneficial for you, and us, and all men.

In St. Peter's, the observers' tribune is under the statue of St. Longinus, directly across from the auditors' tribune (presided over by St. Andrew). Between us, in the nave of the great basilica, the drama of the council unfolds. Let us pretend, for the next 20 minutes, that you are the lay auditors and that I have stepped out of the observers' tribune to come over and visit with you, to comment on what is happening in the council and what this can mean to conscientious and devoted Catholic laymen in the Church tomorrow.

I think I remember when the notion of this assignment may first have stirred in Martin Work's fertile mind. One Sunday evening last October we were together at the Paulist Fathers' house in Rome, and he asked me, point-blank, what I thought about the proposed *Decree on the Apostolate of the Laity,* on docket for debate the following day. In response, I fumbled around for a way to say, as politely as possible, that in its then current form it was quite unimpressive. It then occurred to me that I should balance off that negative judgment with my positive and sincere conviction that in chapter four of the

Constitution on the Church the council had already laid the foundation for an epochal development of the doctrine of the laity in the life and ministry of the Catholic Church. As I recall it, I said something to the effect that this chapter on the laity was the real "sleeper" in the council's documents thus far.

As you may know, the ensuing debate on the apostolate of the laity was largely negative, although not without some notable high moments—among them, Archbishop D'Souza's blunt assertion of the full membership of the laity in the Church, Bishop Leven's intervention on behalf of the true interdependence of clergy and laity, and Bishop Remi De Roo's insistence on the authentic ministries of the laity *in the world*. There was also, of course, Patrick Keagan's fine speech—a layman addressing "the fathers of the council," at their invitation! We must wait until session four to see how well the revisions will turn out. What I most hope for, however, is that the final form of the separate schema on the lay apostolate will rightly grasp and apply the great germinal idea in chapter four of the *Constitution on the Church*. This idea, simply stated, is that the laity *are* "the Church in the modern world"; that the Church's visible presence *in the world* depends upon the laity's making it so. This is one of the four great creative impulses that have emerged in the council thus far—this one, and the notion of "the liturgical act" in the *Constitution on the Sacred Liturgy,* and the doctrine of episcopal collegiality (chapter three of the *Constitution on the Church*), and the charter for "ecumenical dialogue" in the *Decree on Ecumenism* and *Ecclesiam Suam.* Each of these great ideas is basically simple —and none is at all new—but together they are so powerful and profound that they will almost certainly change the face (and the heart and the mind) of the Roman Catholic Church as we have known it for the past century or so.

The council is not yet over—and I must confess to some faint shudders of anxiety over the prospects of reaction, the dangers of what has been called "curial backlash." The *Declaration on Religious Liberty* has not yet been passed—and it stands for many of us as the test of the council's good faith, as far as the practical consequences of the *Decree on Ecumenism* are concerned. There is also the declaration on Catholics and non-Christians—now under massive and, I think, vicious attacks—which must not be scuttled on any ground of so-called "prudence." As a theologian, I am intensely interested in how the *Constitution on Divine Revelation* will come out—for on that depends the future of the dialogue between Catholics and Protestants on the newly fruitful question of Scripture and Tradition. As a moralist, I realize how much is at stake in Schema 13, the *Constitution on the Church in the Modern World.* These items comprise only half of the agenda of session four—though I earnestly hope that the bishops will not feel compelled to "finish" *everything,* whether it is "ripe" or not. We do not need any more unripe decrees like the one on mass communications.

But the foundations of renewal are already laid. The hinge notions are hung. It is now conciliar doctrine that vital worship is truly corporate, not merely private; that the actual leadership of the Church is to be episcopal and not curial; that Christian unity is a dynamic goal, not a gimmick; that *the laity is the Church in the world.* Incarnate these ideas, give them flesh and blood, put them to work with your best intelligence, discipline and devotion, and the renewal of the Church is already underway.

I assume that we may take it for granted that you have read, marked, learned and inwardly digested the text of the *Constitution on the Church,* since it is, almost certainly, the most important single document of Vatican II. If you haven't really read it, you have your own homework still to do, and it ought never be even whispered in Gath or Gilead that a Protestant proferred you a pony for it. It ought to be legitimate, however, for me to offer a few comments on the shape and progression of the doctrine of the Church in its first five chapters—the ones that matter most.

In chapter one, the Church is spoken of as the mysterious *locus* of God's saving work in human history—in and through Jesus Christ, the Divine Word Incarnate. This becomes the basis for our understanding of the sacramental nature of the Church, of the divine environment of our life in the Church, and of the Christocentric character of all our thought about the Church.

In the second chapter, the Church is identified as "the People of God"—the *whole* People of God, clerical *and* lay. Here we are reminded of the fundamental importance of Christian baptism and confirmation as conferring a status upon all the members of the household of faith and providing them with a common ministry—of witness and service in the world. It is made plain that the *cleros* and the *laos*, both together, do God's work in the world, interdependently. The sacrament of orders constitutes the hierarchy, but baptism and confirmation are, together, a sort of ordination to an apostolate of work and witness, which faithful Christians cannot delegate and must not shun.

The third chapter on the hierarchy—in addition to its great central notion of episcopal collegiality—delineates the roles and offices of the sacerdotal ministries of the Church, exhibiting the Church as a sacral society. The stress here is upon the hierarchy as the Church's representative presence in the sacral order—which contradicts in no way the obvious fact that hierarchs are themselves self-evidently human and mundane.

These ideas constitute the premises for chapter four (on the laity) and here the conciliar teaching is clear and momentous. The laity constitute the Church's representative presence in the secular order—and this by divine vocation and human commitment. This is so crucial that I beg leave to quote the key sentences in sections 31-34 (with my own italics added for emphasis):

What specifically characterizes the laity is their secular nature (their situation in the *saeculum*) . . . The laity, by their very *vocation*, place themselves under the rule of God by engaging in temporal affairs and by ordering those affairs according to the will of God. They *live* in the world . . . in all of the secular professions and occupations, . . . in the ordinary circumstances of family and social life—from these the very web of their existence is woven. They are called to this secular existence by God himself, so that if they do their work rightly and are led by the spirit of the Gospel, they do indeed minister to the sanctification of the world *from within*, as a leaven. In such functions they make Christ known to others, especially by the testimony of their lives. . . . Since they are so deeply rooted in all the varieties of temporal affairs, it is their special ministry *to order and to illumine these affairs* in such a way that the secular order itself may give increasing praise to Christ, its creator and redeemer.

. . . All are called to sanctity . . . all have received an equal privilege of faith . . . all share a true equality in respect to the dignity and functions involved in the building up of the Body of Christ.

. . . The laity have Christ for their brother . . . they also have for their brothers those in the sacred ministry . . . but whoever they are, they are called upon, . . . to expend all their energy for the growth of the Church and its continuous sanctification. . . . Through their baptism and confirmation, *all* are *commissioned* to participate in the salvific mission of the Church—and the laity are called in a special way *to make the Church present and operative in those places and circumstances where only through them* can it become "the salt of the earth." Thus, every layman, in virtue of his particular gifts, is a witness to Christ in the world and a living instrument of the mission of the Church itself.

. . . Through their works, prayers and apostolic en-
deavors, their ordinary married and family life, their
daily occupations, etc. . . . *the laity consecrate the world
itself to God.* (Cf. sections 31, 32, 33, 34.)

Here you have the living core of a vital and demanding
concept of the Christian believer, called by God to live
out his Christian faith in the world, through the forms
and activities of secular society—for secular man and for
his salvation. As the hierarchy relate the whole People of
God to the sacral order, so also do the laity relate the
whole People of God to the secular order. Neither is rival
to the other, neither can displace the other, each is inte-
gral to the wholeness of the *populus Dei.* As Section 32
says: "By divine institution, the holy Church is ordered
and governed with a wonderful diversity. All do not proceed by the same path, but *all* are called to sanctity and all
have an equal privilege of receiving faith *as a* [divine]
gift."

Then, as if to focus all these scattered rays of light shed
on so many aspects of the Christian life, chapter five an-
nounces that the call to Christian holiness applies to *all*
the People of God—to the *cleros* in their sacral callings
and to the *laos* in their secular callings—each seeking the
gifts of supernatural charity in those places and in those
tasks wherein their distinctive witness to Christ may be
most effectively manifested.

This doctrine of the ministry of the laity—in, to and
for the world—has almost infinite ramifications, many of
which, I assume, you will be wrestling with in your work-
shops and discussion groups here in this convention, and
afterward in your parishes and dioceses. You will not expect me to propose concrete answers for your own specific
problems, but I would like to list a few of the basic convictions that have formed in my mind as I have pondered
this doctrine of the laity as the Church in the world, and

have tried to consider what it means in terms of the Church's mission.

The first of these is that a layman's earthly calling—his job, his share of the world's work—is the first and fundamental domain in which his Christian witness and service are to be rendered. There is a ghastly misunderstanding in the all too popular notion that a layman's piety is adequately expressed in the "churchwork" that he does in his "spare time," with whatever surplus of energy, talent and money he can scrounge from his "business." Chapter four of the *Constitution on the Church* lays it down, unmistakably, that your most distinctive service to God and your most effective witness to your fellowmen are to be done *in your day's work.* The doing of that work at the top of your powers—in praise of God and to his holy name!—is no more of a routine chore than celebrating the mass is a routine chore for the good priest, and no less an act of piety. The Christian layman's concern for the increase of equity, justice and humanity in his business situation—and for all the people involved in that situation—is at least roughly analogous to the priest's concern for order and equity in his pastoral flock. Part of modern man's damnation roots in the meaninglessness of his *secular* activities and the temptations that beset him in it to ignore or to abuse the good gifts of God, mediated to him through "the things of the world." By the same token, the beginning of his salvation comes with the dawning awareness of the religious import of his divine calling to share in the world's work—meaningful, creative, useful work; work that is, or can be made to be, more significant for *persons* than for *things.* The man who understands his work in the world as his most typical mode of devotion to God—his *unique* service to God's creatures—has a safeguard against the mortal sin of *accidie,* and an immunity from the plague of boredom.

A second corollary of this Vatican doctrine of the laity

is the primacy of the Christian family as *the Church in microcosm*. In this "domestic Church"—as it is spoken of in chapter two—the parents are priests and evangelists to each other and to their children, and in their neighborhood. The implication here—and surely it is a valid one—is that a truly Christian family is the most remarkable of all the forms of Christian witness to the marvels of God's grace in human relations. Success in *this* business is, I think, more difficult and demanding than all but the most heroic careers of the saints, more impressive and effective than all but the greatest preaching, equal in some respects to the martyr's crown. To have done one's part in the formation of such a family must surely rate a brighter crown than almost any other achievement—however matters may stand otherwise in a man's entry in *Who's Who*.

A third corollary of this doctrine of the laity is that the institutional Church—its building and cultus and apparatus—is to be understood as less a hospital than a headquarters; less a refuge than a resource; less an end in itself than a means to a yet higher end: that Christ be made manifest in and for the world's conversion—in this fallen world, so loved by God that he sent his only begotten Son that all in that world who believe on him shall be saved (John 3:16-17).

This special reciprocity between the Church as it opens up to heaven and the Church as it opens out to the world requires a special sort of communication and communion between the sacral and the secular. History reminds us how strong and insidious is the temptation in all interdependent systems for one part to attempt to subordinate the other—not merely by some principle of subsidiarity of function (which is legitimate enough) but in terms of preeminence in status and power. So also in the Church. The representatives of the sacral order have, sometimes, come close to claiming that they *were* the Church. In other times and circumstances the secular order has come close to degrading the hierarchy to the status of spiritual flunkies to secular chieftains. Both these tendencies are equally fatal to the true health and well-being of the Church—and this is why it is so important that the chapter on the laity has charted the golden way between these two extremes.

It is, therefore, my reading of this chapter that it commits you, as Catholic laymen, to a major mutation in your roles and responsibilities in the Church, as these have been defined by your conventional traditions in the past 200 years—although, I should remind you, the chapter is far less an innovation than it is a return to an older, more catholic Catholicism. You are being caught up in a transition from the erstwhile role indicated by the old bromide about "believe, pray, pay and obey" to the tasks of a complex program of co-operation and consultation in the life and work of the Church. But even this, as I am willing to repeat almost endlessly, is not an end in itself. Your real goal transcends the matter of your *status* and centers on your distinctive *function:* the effective manifestation of *the Church in the world.* No part of this transition will be simple, automatic, perfectly harmonious. The hierarchy, in their power of ruling and judging and sanctifying, have normal and appropriate "channels" for communicating their mind and will to the faithful. But what sort of patterns of communication have the *laos* for conveying their "mind" to the *cleros*—especially in those crucial cases where there is not one "mind" but many? One has only to think of the current hubbub about vernacular liturgies—or the odd and mercifully short history of Father De Pauw's Catholic Traditionalist Society. But we might better take something far closer to the heart of the matter.

There is, as you know, a schema before the council on the Church in the modern world—a sort of programmatic charter for the laity as we have seen it set forth in the chapter on the laity. In this schema there are eight great issues singled out for emphasis: the dignity of man, the meaning of human vocation, the relations between church and state, world poverty and economic and social justice, the dignity of marriage and the family, the religious significance of human culture, the solidarity of the family of nations, and a planet peaceful enough for man to survive on its surface. But if, as I have argued, the laity is the Church in the modern world, then Schema 13 must reflect the realistic possibilities of the high professional competence of many laymen in one or another of these fields. It is not merely that the clergy and the laity should discuss these issues and exchange ideas. It is also a question of how the laity propose to become parts of the Christian *solutions* to these problems rather than continue as parts of the problems themselves. And even more—and I gather that this is what the council really intends—this doctrine implies that the Church must utilize the vocational and professional talents of all its people, as they may bear upon the facets and dimensions of the Church's presence in the modern world. This means, in turn, that the laity must be prepared to respond and, where appropriate, take graceful initiatives of their own.

But you must be very clear on one point: no good end will be served by the mere dislodging of ecclesiastical power, or the shifting of it from one place to another. God save you from a false clericalization of the laity! Believe me, laicism is no better for the Church than clericalism—and I ought to know, for many of us in the Protestant traditions have had to learn *this* lesson the hard way. What is required of you is a profound and stable understanding of the mutuality of the sacral and the secular and, in consequence, the responsible exercise of Christian liberty in free but grateful commitment to new levels of communication and service in the Church and, through the Church, to the world.

Thus, one of the nuclear notions of the *Constitution on the Church* is that the *cleros* and the *laos* serve each other as, together, they serve the mission of the Church, which is the salvation of the world. But the *laos* is scarcely competent for its ministry of witness and service unless it is in the closest true fellowship with the hierarchy, and vice versa. The development of this fellowship will have all sorts of implications: new conceptions of the apostolic formation of the Catholic laity, new roles for the Catholic intellectual and scientist, new self-understandings by Catholic business leaders, industrialists and statesmen of their religious duties *in the world.*

Vatican II has gotten the bishops accustomed to, and generally grateful for, their *periti.* There was, of course, that story running around Rome last fall about the bishop who had no *peritus.* When asked why, he explained that he would feel embarrassed to have a *peritus* much cleverer than he and that, after diligent search, he still hadn't found one that wasn't. These experts—usually theologians—have provided the bishops with professional counsel and commentary, sometimes, with nicely phrased Latin translations of their speeches. But normally, they have not presumed to cross the border between *counsel* and *judgment.* This idea of the effective use of "lay *periti*" might profitably work in a diocese or in a local parish. Bishop Leven made an intervention to this general effect last October. Bishop Reed is planning a "little Vatican Council" for his diocese (Oklahoma) next year; other bishops have done various things along this line, though usually on a rather episodic and unsystematic basis. Now, it seems to me, the idea can really be developed into a program and made to work—always mindful that what you are concerned with is the *Church's presence in and for the world.* In this sense, chapter four will be the doctrinal foundation and cross reference both for

Schema 13 and for the *Decree on the Apostolate of the Laity.*

In closing, I have a mild word of warning to you, based on our Protestant experiences, in which we've tended to bend the bow the other way. If the Vatican's doctrine of the laity ever comes to be used by over-zealous laymen to muzzle and tame your priests in their prophetic criticism of the standing order or, alternatively, if it should ever encourage the notion that you have some rightful power over your priests and bishops because of your hands on the purse strings, then you will have tattered the whole splendid vision of the People of God and will have tragically failed the Church in your greatest hour of opportunity and challenge.

But this need not happen. It must not happen. If we are to look ahead toward some convergence in our growth toward Christian unity—toward what Pope Paul calls "the recomposition of Christian unity"—one of the most powerful incentives and guides to us all must be the development of an effective and authentic laymen's movement that really understands both the differences and the interdependencies of the sacral and the secular in the Christian community, that really takes its ministry in the world and its mission to the world in all seriousness, that wipes away the Protestant bogey of Catholics as gullible men stumbling under a mindless yoke of priestcraft and yet also avoids the Protestant travesty of ministers at the mercy of their rich and powerful "lay leaders."

The Christian unity that we seek is in a Church that exhibits Christ to the world in the manifold witness of Christian men and women doing their daily work to the glory of God, in their family life, in their neighborhoods, in their civic duties and in all of their temporal responsibilities. You have the charter for this in chapter four of your *Constitution on the Church.* Show us the way, and if we fail to follow, or fail to find our own equivalent, then the judgment of history on us will be all the more ironic: that the Romans recovered what Protestantism once had and then lost because we were too sure that it was ours by divine right!

But it may be that we will not fail, either. My dream and hope and daily prayer is that we shall take heart from you and be ready to meet you at that joining of the ways which God has prepared for us all sometime, somewhere, in his good Providence. Meanwhile, and at the very least, read well and take heed of the signs of your times. Your tide is now rising to that sort of flood which must be taken at its peak if you are to rise to the challenge, the need and the possibilities of your service in Christ's mission to and for this broken world!

CHAPTER 10

LIBERTY DEFERRED:
A CRISIS IN VATICAN II

June, 1965

The only portions of my diary that have been published thus far appeared as the lead article in the summer issue (1965) of *The Southwest Review*, the literary quarterly published by the SMU Press. It is a running commentary on the vicissitudes of the *Declaration on Religious Liberty* throughout session three, plus a blow-by-blow account of the now famous brouhaha of Thursday, November 19.

I had an incomparable observation post from which to watch the whole affair and I had a passionate interest in seeing and recording all of it I possibly could, both because it seemed plain that this was a tremendous crisis and also because I was so deeply convinced that the council's ecumenical commitments would stand or fall by its disposition of this issue.

Now that the business has had its happy ending—with an even better declaration than we would have had if the bishops had accepted the 1964 version—it is possible to suggest that I was over-excited and that I overplayed the tensions and conflict. But one must insist that the outcome *was* in genuine doubt *then*—and if I exaggerated the objective realities (as these appear in retrospect), it still is true that these diary excerpts are an honest mirror of the intensity of my interest and anxieties at the time and on the spot.

Here, then, is a sample of "instant history"—an unretouched account of the most dramatic single passage in the complex story of Vatican II.

Wednesday, September 23, 1964

The first two speeches today concluded the discussion of the role and office of bishops and opened the way for debate on the *Declaration on Religious Liberty,* which had caused such a row when it was sidetracked last year by a parliamentary maneuver. Bishop Emile De Smedt (Bruges) presented the *relatio* (introduction), explaining the aims and issues in the new text now before the bishops. Then followed nine cardinals and a single bishop. Cardinal Ruffini (Palermo) was as immobilist as ever and argued that governments have the right to establish and maintain the true religion and that error and false religion have no rights, ecclesiastical or civil. Cardinal Quiroga (Santiago de Compostela, Spain) spoke out of the Spanish situation and pointed out how such an ambiguous text would be badly misunderstood in a Catholic country. He reminded the bishops that the Roman Church had consistently denounced liberalism, modernism and secularism and then declared that this schema was a product of that same liberal, modernist, secular viewpoint that already stood condemned. "How," he asked, "are we to justify this inconsistency?" Cardinal Léger (Montreal) approved the document and argued for liberty as a human right grounded in natural law.

All of this was predictable, but then came the bombshell. Cardinal Cushing (Boston) took the floor and in a voice that sounded like an old-fashioned revivalist roaring at the crowd, he paraphrased the American Declaration of Independence to the effect that the Catholic Church ought also to have a decent respect for the opinions of mankind, that Catholics must grant to others what they have steadfastly demanded for themselves, that "religious freedom (defined as the immunity from all coercion in religious affairs) is a necessary means, willed by God, by which men can seek God, can find him, can serve him." He concluded by appealing to Pope John XXIII, insisting that this declaration is simply an extension of the teaching of *Pacem in Terris.*

This was the first time that Cardinal Cushing has spoken in the council and nothing like this strident, drawling voice was ever heard in these precincts. It was also the first time that an all-out liberal doctrine of religious liberty has ever been argued so bluntly by so high an official in so solemn a setting. There was a confidence in the man's tone —a manifest determination that this council must strike a blow for liberty—and it made for a very dramatic moment indeed. "In this declaration the Church must show itself to the entire world as the champion of liberty, of human liberty and of civil liberty, specifically in the matter of religion." I found it startling and wonderful, for here at last the American experience has made its full impact upon the Roman Catholic Church. Nothing like it has happened before and nothing like it could have happened much earlier than today.

Then came Cardinal Bueno (Seville) and we were back once more in the Mediterranean mentality. He could approve the abstract principle of religious liberty but found insuperable difficulty in passing from principle to practice, in politics and society. Surely it ought to be lawful, he said, to prohibit the spread of error when this can do harm to those who are seeking to profess the true Christian faith.

Now it was Meyer's (Chicago) turn, and it was interesting to see how many bishops came down from their seats to crowd around the crossing of the basilica, where they could see Meyer up close. He sits on the far right end of the podium where they have the council presidents. This man is in charge of the largest Catholic diocese in America, and it is plain that he is being heard with very great respect by the moderates and the uncommitted, for he is himself a known moderate and a confidant of Pope Paul VI.

He was followed by Cardinal Ritter (St. Louis), and this marks the first time that three American cardinals have ever spoken in the council in a single day. McIntyre (Los Angeles) is still in the hospital (he collapsed during the opening ceremonies, September 14), and Spellman (New York) has not yet come over—so it turned out that all the American cardinals present spoke at one time and to the same effect. Ritter's intervention was in some ways the strangest of the three, because he argued that since religious liberty is a self-evident good, the declaration ought to be quite simple, with no argumentation attached—for if you argue about it, you imply that it is an open question. He feared that the council could get hung up on the question as to whether the reasons given were adequate or not. What was really demanded was a forthright declaration that would be categorical and unequivocal. Ritter was followed by the most progressive cardinal in South America (Silva Henriquez of Santiago, Chile) speaking for 58 Latin American bishops. His main point was that it was high time Latin America had a doctrine of religious liberty that would stop the wrong kind of proselytism, among both Roman Catholics and others. He said that this would mean that the number of conversions in some localities might very well drop, but the quality would increase—and he and his colleagues would rather have it that way than as at present.

Ottaviani (the Holy Office) concluded for the cardinals and seemed to me to be paving the way for a decent, though grudging, retreat. He objected to the notion of "honoring" the consciences of men who have a false religion ("respect" is nearer a literal translation of the text). He pointed out that such a declaration would invalidate the existing concordats which the Vatican has with various governments. He denounced the section on proselytism and generally expressed his distaste for the whole idea. "Let us take care not to arm our adversaries," he warned. But the cause was lost and he knew it. The atmosphere of St. Peter's was electric with the sense of an historic moment that had arrived in the fullness of its time.

But there was a further bit of drama to be added. Bishop Cekada (Skoplje, Yugoslavia) spoke out as a martyr (the literal meaning of "witness") on behalf of religious liberty in those lands where militant atheism controls the public sector of the press and education and mass communications. He wanted the council to appeal to the United Nations to issue a declaration "proclaiming solemnly the obligation of respecting religious freedom in any land or nation, including all forms of religious activity." It should stress particularly the dimensions of the problem falling within the public sector of society: freedom of worship, freedom to have schools, freedom to own buildings for religious purposes, freedom to conduct public religious ceremonies.

There was no mistaking the fact that he was speaking in bold defiance of his own government, laying himself open to savage persecution when he returns. I find this sort of cold courage genuinely impressive. He actually ran overtime, but the moderator (Cardinal Suenens, Brussels) was aware of the pathos of the situation and did not cut him off. He did, however, ask him to conclude and Bishop Cekada replied, *"Si, grazie, subito!"* Literally, this would mean, "Yes, thank you—*immediately.*" In normal Italian usage, however, it means, "In a little while," or "presently." This caused a friendly laugh.

All told, we had a great morning, and I'm deeply grateful to have been here to see and hear it all. If and when this declaration is passed, September 23 will be remembered in the history books.

Thursday, September 24

Today we were treated to a nearly solid phalanx of *immobilisti*—a long lesson in classical Spanish and Italian ecclesiology, with its feudal conceptions of church and state. Even the exceptions—Cardinal Koenig (Vienna) and Bishop Primeau (New Hampshire) —failed to dispel my feeling that St. Peter's is haunted by ghosts—shades of the Holy Inquisition and of the *ius gladii* (the Church's right to use the sword against heretics)! Over and over it was said that error has no rights, that the Catholic Church is entitled to freedom when it is in the minority but has no obligation to be tolerant when it is in the majority, because it professes the one true religion and is the guardian of all truth. As my students know, I normally think of the Protestant Reformation as a twin tragedy shot through with ill temper and bigotry on both sides. But after this concentrated dose of Roman triumphalism, I begin to think that one's only recourse against it would have to be open revolt. At least, I begin to understand Wesley's implacable detestation of "papacy"—identified, as it was for him, with religious persecution. . . .

Friday, September 25

The debate on religious liberty continued this morning and might have gone on throughout the day and next Monday, too—for there were 26 speakers signed up on the secretary general's list. What happened was that a curious little deal was worked out that allowed Bishop Carlo Colombo, Pope Paul VI's personal theologian, to conclude the debate, prior to a vote on cloture. It took some fancy footwork to get this timed just right and this was interesting to watch. About 11 o'clock, "Uncle Pericles" (Archbishop Pericle Felici, the secretary general) went up to Cardinal Bea's place (in the cardinals' tribune, across the aisle from the observers; Bea is chairman of the Secretariat for Promoting Christian Unity). It turned out, afterward, that Felici was asking Bea to introduce his *relatio* on the declaration on Catholic-Jewish relations today— rather than wait till next week, as had been planned. I noticed that, for the next 40 minutes, Bea was quite busy with his papers and notes. Meanwhile, Uncle Pericles had issued two warnings to the bishops to return to their seats from the coffee bars, but this is something of a routine of his. At 11:50 Bishop Colombo was recognized to speak; when he had finished, Cardinal Suenens (the moderator) announced that the bishops would now vote for or against cloture. This unexpected vote was affirmative, but not at all unanimous, for it meant cutting off about 15 bishops whose names had already been announced.

Suenens then announced, to the surprise of many, that Cardinal Bea would now give the *relatio* on the declaration on Catholic-Jewish relations—because, said he, his eminence was leaving on the morrow for Patras, heading the delegation that was returning the relic of St. Andrew's head to the Orthodox cathedral there. Bea's presentation was superb, as always—I just put a homemade translation of it in my files.

The point to this little drama is that Colombo's intervention was improvised in order to suggest, *indirectly,* that the Pope himself is in favor of this declaration, suitably grounded; that he wished to have his point of view intimated to the council, thus avoiding the excessive force of a direct papal intervention. It was, so to say, an instance of the Pope's acting on the principle of collegiality. Colombo's arguments seemed to me an improvement on the arguments in the present text and will undoubtedly be used in its revision. They neatly undercut the arguments of the Spaniards and the Italians—yet Colombo is himself Italian and a *peritus* to an Italian pope. If and when this matter is settled, this intervention of Colombo's will have been important, for it is bound to reassure the hesitant and the uncommitted. Those who really believe in religious liberty will vote for it on principle. Those who were waiting for a sign from above now have one. This leaves only the hard core of the convinced opposition with their *non-placets*. This was a crucial turn of affairs—and should be remembered when the story can be told in full.

Friday, October 16

Tonight I got a pretty full account of the latest crisis in the perils of the *Declaration on Religious Liberty*. It seems that last Friday, October 9, the Secretariat for Promoting Christian Unity received two letters from Archbishop Felici, "on higher authority," suggesting that a review committee be established to inspect the texts of the declarations on religious liberty and on the Jews. This committee would consist of two curial officials, Michael Cardinal Browne and Archbishop Marcel Lefebvre; Father Aniceto Fernandez (governor-general of the Dominican Order) ; and Bishop Carlo Colombo—three *immobilisti* and one progressive. This bold threat to the two declarations caused a great hue and cry all over town.

On Sunday, Cardinal Frings (Cologne) and ten other cardinals got together and addressed a letter to the Pope complaining of this procedure. The same day, the Canadian bishops also had a conference and resolved to protest if it should become necessary. The American bishops whom I met seemed annoyed but did not believe anything serious would come of it.

Apparently what has happened is that the Arab states were putting fantastic pressure on the Vatican Secretary of State, who then got Felici to help pull this chestnut out of the fire by going to the Pope and suggesting this review committee as a way of expediting the council's business and of insuring harmony on these controversial issues. In this he was supported by Ottaviani and other *immobilisti*. The Pope apparently agreed to the proposal, with the stipulation that it must also be acceptable to the Secretariat for Promoting Christian Unity, which has charge of these items.

Meanwhile, Bea had called his team into a huddle and, politely but firmly, accepted the proposal *provided* that the committee's role be understood as consultative and the Secretariat retain jurisdiction over both declarations. By the middle of the week the palace revolution had been squelched—a desperate move, illustrating the mood of men who are prepared to do reckless things in order to save the Church from the ruin they see impending.

Monday, November 9

I heard today that they have the *Declaration on Religious Liberty* ready for printing and that it may be in the hands of the bishops before the week is out.

Tuesday, November 10

One of the American bishops told me today that the theological commission has turned down the *Declaration on Religious Liberty* by a vote of 16 to 13. He thinks this may delay its appearance. Other rumors have it that this vote has been overmatched by a thumping majority in the Secretariat for Promoting Christian Unity, which has primary jurisdiction, and that the coordinating commission has decided that the council should vote on the question as to whether the present text forms an acceptable basis for further amendment. Otherwise, the theological commission would have had a veto over a crucial issue that lies outside its jurisdiction (but not its interest!).

Thursday, November 12

The word today is that the texts of the declarations on religious liberty and on Christian-non-Christian relations are at the printers but that the theological commission is now working on a new proposal to annex the text on Christian-non-Christian relations to chapter two of the *Constitution on the Church*. They *never* give up!

Wednesday, November 18

Yesterday we finally got the printed text of the new version of *Religious Liberty* and it prompts an uneasy feeling that we are in for trouble. Today we got the *Declaration on the Relationship of the Church to Non-Christian Religions* and my anxieties have increased. Each has been extensively revised from the earlier texts and the calendar is crowding us very close (adjournment date, Saturday November 21). Distracted as I was, however, I was greatly impressed by Cardinal Léger's great speech on intellectual freedom as the basis of sound Christian education—and I was also pleased to see the concluding chapters of the *Constitution on the Church* voted through. In the long run, *this* document will be seen as this council's most important *theological* achievement.

At the end of the session the gage of battle was thrown down. Felici, speaking for the moderators and the presidents, informed the bishops that because of complaints about the schema on religious liberty—that it had been handed to them too late to be studied carefully, that it was what amounted to a new text, that there were many questions of conscientious doubt about it in the minds of many fathers—there will be a preliminary vote tomorrow on the question as to whether there shall be a formal vote at this session. You could feel the house go tense; but I have no doubt that they'll vote to vote, overwhelmingly.

Thursday, November 19

Today disaster struck. The course of true love never did run smooth, nor does that of a reforming council. When I was going up the aisle of St. Peter's this morning, I noticed a group of bishops concentrated around Bishop Luigi Carli (Segni, Italy—an extreme *immobilisto*) but supposed that they were merely taking counsel as to how to muster their votes for the preliminary ballot on whether to vote to vote on religious liberty. Then, directly after mass, Carli came to the Secretary General's desk (some eight feet from my place in the observers' tribune) and handed Felici a letter with many signatures. Felici took this up to Cardinal Tisserant (senior president of the council *and* papal legate). Tisserant came back over to the secretary's desk for discussion, where they were joined by Cicognani (Secretary of State and president of the co-ordinating commission) and Roberti (the parliamentarian of the College of Cardinals and of the council). At this point I realized that all this had something to do with this preliminary vote, but even then it did not cross my mind that the thing could be simply canceled. I knew, of course, that article 30 of the *Ordo* (the Council's equivalent of Roberts' *Rules of Order*) says that new texts may not be voted upon until they have been debated, but I supposed that the council was free to suspend its own rules, if it chose to do so by some majority fraction (two-thirds or even three-fourths) ; and I felt confident that there would be such a majority. . . .

From here on, I'd best transcribe the blow-by-blow account of the events of the next two and a half hours, just as I scribbled them down in my notebook. 10:08—and Doepfner (Munich, cardinal moderator for the day) introduces the debate on Christian education. Seven speakers are listed but now I am too absorbed in this other business to listen to them very closely. Under our tribune, the conference continues between Felici and Ottaviani, who has come over from the cardinals' tribune. Now Lercaro (Bologna, and one of the moderators) gets into it with Tisserant and Felici. Tisserant shrugs his shoulders at Lercaro, who appears to be protesting something or other. Felici is visibly unhappy; he is not clowning now as he sometimes does when handling a hot potato.

Lercaro goes back to the moderators' table and talks to Doepfner and Koenig. Tisserant and Felici continue. Now comes Ruffini from his place on the far right of the presidents' podium to get his oar in. Tisserant goes back to the podium and tackles Frings. Frings shrugs his shoulders as if to say: "If you want to, go ahead, but count me out."

10:12. Tisserant turns now to Caggiano (Buenos Aires), then to Wyszynski (Warsaw), and then to Alfrink (Utrecht). He's canvassing the presidents, getting their vote on something. Caggiano and Wyszynski have apparently agreed; Alfrink has disagreed. Meanwhile, Lercaro has gone up to Bea (cardinals' tribune) and they are in deep conversation, with Lercaro carrying the ball.

Now Tisserant goes to Gilroy (Sydney, Australia), to Ruffini, and then to Siri (Genoa), but not to Meyer, on Ruffini's right. Instead, he comes back to Tappouni (Patriarch of Antioch). I think this means he has his majority in the presidents—without Meyer! At any rate, Meyer and Siri and Ruffini are having a very animated three-cornered argument. Lercaro is still talking to Bea, with Felici looking up at them, apprehensive (I think) as to what they may be cooking up. They finish at 10:22—ten full minutes of it. . . .

Now Tisserant and Felici have gone over to the moderators' desk and Doepfner lets fall a pause after Bishop Okoye (Port Harcourt, Nigeria) gets through speaking. This is the first time I recall any such break in the steady stream of speakers—which goes to show how distracted everybody is. After a couple of minutes, Doepfner introduces Bishop Abed (Tripoli, Lebanon), but the conference at the moderators' table continues. Felici returns to the secretary's desk, looking grim, and begins to talk to Morcillo (Archbishop of Madrid and an undersecretary), and Tisserant goes to the moderators for another five minutes of conference. Now he too comes to the secretary's desk, to Villot (coadjutor of Lyons and an undersecretary) —grimmer than usual, which is considerable. The moderators are now talking together, *molto agitato*—and I get the impression that they are not going to go along with the presidents in whatever is being decided.

Tisserant shows Villot a paper with some sort of memorandum on it—I think it must be the announcement that they've been hassling over. Villot reads it and then sits down to dash off a note. Léger rises from his seat and comes down to the presidents' desk, but approaches no one in particular.

Now Morcillo and Krol (Archbishop of Philadelphia, another undersecretary) are in animated conversation. The atmosphere in the *aula* is getting edgy; everybody seems to realize that some very tricky business is going on. Doepfner now calls for cloture on the discussion of Christian education and it passes handily. Felici returns with the final ballot on the *Constitution on the Church* as a whole—which has only 10 negative votes!—and suggests that the bishops have a right to congratulate themselves on this great achievement (as indeed they have!). But then Fernandez the Dominican, in the name of 70 bishops, rises to continue the clotured discussion on Christian education (the *Ordo* provides for this). Now I see why Doepfner wanted to cut it off when he did, for Fernandez has launched into a eulogy on St. Thomas Aquinas as the model for theological education, which takes the form of a counterattack against all criticisms of Thomism such as we have been hearing, notably in Léger's speech.

A *peritus* sitting next to me reports that some of the

Latin American bishops have distributed mimeographed lists of *modi* (amendments) to the *Declaration on Religious Liberty* and these are already for subscription and signature. All a bishop does is sign his name and there is his *modus* made up for him in advance. Also, Bishop Carli has distributed a thousand *modi* against the declaration, asking the bishops to join with him in blocking this vote—so as to open the argument up all over again. What looked hopeful yesterday is now put back in jeopardy. Léger, looking glum, nevertheless breaks into a grin at Fernandez' ferocious attack upon the critics of Thomism, in which he is being singled out for special treatment.

Doepfner calls Fernandez to time and the bishops break out into applause, which is highly irregular—also, I think, unprecedented since the first session when Alfrink called Ottaviani to time. Fernandez concludes in a huff. Felici and Krol are in an argument. Felici shrugs and looks up to Tisserant as if the moment of truth has come. And so it has. 11:00 a.m. Doepfner introduces Cardinal Tisserant, dean of the Sacred College and chairman of the council of presidents, who has an announcement to make. (Notice that the moderators are not mentioned; they have dealt themselves out of it.) Now Tisserant: "Many fathers have objected that there is not sufficient time to consider the new text on religious liberty and to formulate mature judgments before being called upon to vote, as had been announced yesterday. This is especially the case since the text presents a new format, as is admitted by the Secretariat for Promoting Christian Unity. It seems proper to the presidency [a majority of them, but not all!] that this cannot be decided by a vote of a general congregation. There will not, therefore, be a vote. What is allowed is the presentation of the *relatio*—and then there will be full discussion of a new text in the fourth session of the council. Those fathers who wish to do so are asked to send in written observations before January 31, 1965."

This announcement was greeted by wild but quite scattered applause at this upper end of the *aula* and a shocked silence down at the far end where the younger bishops sit (they're seated in the order of their episcopal seniority). The *immobilisti* have succeeded in thwarting the manifest will of the majority who are not going to be allowed to vote on whether to vote. This leaves the question wide open, with further chances for the diehards to wreck the project, by fair means or foul.

Public reaction to this will be furious and at least partly justified. The opponents of religious liberty reject the notion that a majority vote would settle the issue. This is the naked face of that authoritarianism we Protestants were taught to fear in Rome—and that I had come to think was pretty well passé. Even now, I believe this action gives a false picture of the council as a whole—but there's no doubt that these people are so fully convinced that they are trustees of the truth that they regard it as their right and duty to protect that truth from the misguided majority, however huge.

De Smedt is now introduced to present his *relatio*. Here is one of the great orators of the council, sounding as if he scarcely knew what to say—and small wonder. It is now 11:10 and a flurry of activity is beginning over in the south transept. There is Meyer towering in the midst of a group of American bishops like a general marshaling and deploying his troops. De Smedt finishes his presentation. There is a thunderous applause from all over the *aula*, and the "diaspora" (Uncle Pericles' name for the bishops who are out of their seats) as well. Doepfner interrupts; the applause dies; and then it swells again in a new wave. These men are upset. Having been thwarted from voting by ballot, they are now voting with their hands, defying the management in the bargain.

Now one sees sheets being passed out—petitions to overrule Tisserant—and they are being circulated through the

hall brazenly and even by the *assignatores locuti* (ushers),
which is quite clearly against the rules. Yet neither Tisserant nor Felici makes any move to stop it—although last
year they intervened personally in a far less serious matter
and snatched unauthorized papers out of people's hands.
Now they simply sit and watch in what looks to me like
glowering fury.

What happened was that it took less than 20 minutes
after Tisserant's announcement for the American bishops
to draft a petition to the Pope, get it typed on Felici's type-
writer and run off on the Secretariat's multigraph ma-
chine—this, I gather, was Krol's contribution to the cause
—and hundreds of copies are being distributed throughout the basilica. In English it would go like this—"Holy
Father: reverently but with great urgency, with greater
urgency, and with the greatest urgency, we ask that a vote
on the *Declaration on Religious Liberty* be allowed before the end of this session, lest the trust of the world,
both Christian and non-Christian, be forfeited."

This is the first time that the Americans have been really touched at a point that deeply matters to them. This,
therefore, may be the day when they have become fully
involved in this council. If so, this defeat will be only a
temporary setback and the reactionaries will have finally
overreached themselves. . . .

It is well to remember that the most crucial period of a
revolution is that time after its first successes have been
achieved, when the original architects of the revolution
become overconfident and open the door to reaction—or
else lose their grip on the forces they have let loose and so
unleash the adventurers who profit from confusion. The
progressives' cause was going swimmingly in this session.
Their majorities were tremendous; their gains were
greater than had been expected. But now they have been
booby-trapped, not so much by a deep-laid conspiracy as
by the brilliant exploitation of a parliamentary technical-

ity. These diehards are masters of improvisation. They saw an opening, they struck like lightning and scored a knockout; before the progressive majority knew what was happening, they were on the ropes. . . .

After adjournment, I heard that Cardinals Meyer, Ritter and Léger were going to see the Pope this afternoon with the petition. A first report was that there were 900 signatures on it; later estimates have taken this up as high as 1,400. Tonight I was told by a quite reliable source that their visit had been fruitless, for the Pope, thus confronted, had said that he was unwilling to overrule a decision of the council of presidents—although just yesterday he had overruled the Secretariat for Promoting Christian Unity in the matter of the text of the *Decree on Ecumenism,* and has made other unilateral decisions resolving conflicts between subsidiary authorities. What was more crucially involved, I would guess, is the prestige of Cardinal Tisserant, the dean of the Sacred College. If the Pope were publicly to embarrass Tisserant, the repercussions would be serious, and extremely awkward. . . .

Now the breach between the curia and the pastoral episcopate has been widened and embittered on both sides. Meyer and Tisserant are at loggerheads, the Americans have offended some of the Europeans by their aggressive tactics, the *immobilisti* have been encouraged to hope that they can win by getting the Pope into their corner. It is the first time in the council that the two sides have maneuvered themselves past the point of rational compromise.

Friday, November 20

. . . Tisserant rose to state that since a number of bishops had been disappointed by the failure to vote on the religious liberty schema, they had petitioned the Pope to bring the declaration to the floor for a vote today. He wished to report that the Pope's judgment was that the council presidency in agreeing to delay a vote to permit further study of the declaration had acted in accordance with the *Ordo*. This delay, the Cardinal said, was proof of the presidency's respect for the conscientious concerns of those who had appealed to the *Ordo*. However, he continued, the declaration will come up for discussion and a vote at the next session of the council and, if possible, will have priority on the agenda. This sounds like a promise and now there will be at least a thousand bishops who are determined to see that it is honored. . . .

CHAPTER 11

REFORMATION DAY UPDATED

September, 1965

Yet another chance to interpret Vatican II to my fellow Methodists came shortly after the National Council of Catholic Men address—in an invitation from Dr. Edwin H. Maynard of *The Methodist Story,* a monthly magazine devoted to program-planning for local pastors and church leaders. It had occurred to Dr. Maynard that the council's experiment in "Reformation Roman-Style" had a definite bearing on the anniversaries of "Reformation Protestant-Style" that are still cherished and observed. I heartily agreed, of course, and the article was published in the *Story* in September, 1965.

Catholics need occasionally to try to understand the force and persistence of Protestant feelings of reverence toward the titans of their 16th-century Reformation plus their concomitant antipathies toward the Church of Rome and "popery." These anti-Roman attitudes were further scarred in the 17th century by the ghastly Wars of Religion and then fixated in the 19th century by the wide consensus that Rome's ultimate goal, in *every* country, was *political control*—which could also be spelled p-a-p-a-l t-y-r-a-n-n-y. Thus, for four centuries, we have been proud of and inspired by the faithfulness and fortitude of our Protestant martyrs and oblivious of the Roman Catholics we had "crowned" upon occasion. In our history books, it was the "Good Queen Bess" and "Bloody Mary" (although their respective scores in victims added up to something close to a tie).

Reformation Day (October 31) has long served as a single memorial focus for the recapitulation of this whole history—with its entail of pride and fear, of reverence and rededication. Often it has also served as a sort of test-occasion of one's religious loyalty like a patriotic rally on the Fourth of July. Anyone seriously questioning the anti-Catholic assumptions of such observances was open to the suspicion of being crypto-Catholic—or worse. I've lost count of the half-humorous comments I've had about *my* dalliances with the Romans.

And yet it is clearly no part of the ecumenical program for any group to disparage or discard their own heritage—and the worst service Protestants could render to the real goals of Christian unity would be to forget or to repudiate the great central convictions of the Reformation—which are "catholic" in the sense that they belong to the apostolic message in its patristic understanding which is still the closest approach to "the primordial Christian universal" we have. Besides, some of the creative emphases in Vatican II resonate with these ideas—and go back to the same sources.

It used to be that the program for Reformation Day planned itself—and, like all Gaul, it was divided into three parts. One part was *historical:* something about Luther's nailing the 95 Theses to the *Schlosskirchentür* at Wittenberg; something about the parlous state of the papal Church; and, when the service was under Methodist auspices, something about John Wesley's contribution to the continuing reformation in Protestantism, etc., etc. A second part had to be *theological:* something about the cardinal tenets of the Reformation (salvation by faith alone, the authority of Scripture, the priesthood of all believers, etc.), something about "the Protestant principle" and the blessings of religious liberty, something about the errors of Rome, etc., etc. The third part was *liturgical,* the minimum core of which consisted in the lusty singing of "A Mighty Fortress Is Our God."

Of late years, it has also been the fashion to make of Reformation Day an "ecumenical occasion," with some visible act of recognition of our "spiritual unity" with other Christians—which was to say, other Protestants. In this connection, it was not thought inappropriate to remind ourselves of our ancient estrangement from the Roman Catholics and of our four centuries of heroic conflict, symbolized by Luther's "Here I stand . . ." at Worms or that grim Reformation Monument in Geneva. It was in Reformation Day services (though not exclusively there) that I learned about the Catholics' idolatry in their masses and Marian devotions, of their ruthless slaughter of Protestants, of their political duplicity and secret ambitions to subvert free government in the name of papal absolutism. It was afterward and elsewhere, that I learned of the sizable army of *Catholic* martyrs, done in by Protestants, of *Catholic* advocates of "a free church in a free state," and of the tragic mischief wrought by anti-Catholic prejudice in American religious history, continuing down to the present day.

This traditional format for Reformation Day—of, by and for Protestants—went well enough so long as the Romans kept to themselves and to their own *Counter*-Reformation ways. But what are we to do, now, in this new era of Vatican II, when so many of our comfortable old stereotypes are in the process of being dissolved? If we are to commemorate our forefathers' Reformation, four centuries ago, we can scarcely ignore the fact that the Romans are in the midst of a reformation of their own, here and now, and around the world—that same Roman Church that was, as we so often said, "unreformed and irreformable." Either they are perpetrating a gigantic hoax or our Roman Catholic brethren are in the opening stages of a radically new chapter in their history—and in our histories, too! They have begun to close out the old era of their Counter-Reformation; they have launched vast changes in their patterns of worship and polity; they have promulgated a *Decree on Ecumenism* that turns a decisive corner for them, and for us; by October 31 they will have voted on two epoch-making declarations (on Religious Liberty and on the Jews). In short, they are in the midst of one of the most dramatic (and audacious) experiments in church renewal in a thousand years. Clearly, in such a situation, a routine repetition of Reformation Day, "old style," would be archaic and inept. On the other hand, we can scarcely cancel the calendar; we need not apologize for Luther and Calvin and Wesley; we cannot pretend that four centuries of alienation can be glossed over, between newfound friends, as if their residues were not still with us. What then to do? This is what I call a *providential* problem—namely, an unsought and unexpected crisis that opens a new frontier of significant opportunity.

There can't be many Catholics or Protestants left in America who haven't already shared in some sort of service symbolizing this new "spirit of Vatican II": from Boston to San Francisco, to San Antonio, to St. Louis, to Lake Junaluska, to South Bend, to Albuquerque, to Nevada, to Missouri. I've been in a hundred of them myself, and the end is not yet. There are now several places where Catholic churches have joined local Councils of Churches. In New Mexico, Archbishop Davis has led his whole archdiocese into the state council. In Dallas, two overlapping parishes (St. Pius X and St. Stephen's) organized a mass meeting in which Bishop Gorman and I reviewed the *Decree on Ecumenism*—and SMU and the University of Dallas co-sponsored a service of common worship during last January's Octave of Unity. Last June in Spokane, Washington, Pacific Northwest Annual Conference delegates stayed in the dormitories of Gonzaga University, a Roman Catholic school. Some meetings were held in the Central Christian Church; evening sessions were at the Masonic Temple; and the ordination service was at the Episcopal Cathedral of St. John. Jesuit fathers of Gonzaga said a 6:45 a.m. "mass for Methodists" and some 300 conference delegates came. The priests responded by sending a delegation to the Methodist ordination service. And so the stories go, on and on, and from all over.

The first practical corollary of all this is that Reformation Day, 1965 is the obvious occasion for reporting and interpreting this new situation to our people. And what could be more appropriate in this reporting and interpreting than the help of a competent and informed Roman Catholic? Don't ask him to talk about *our* reformation; what about *his?* What does it feel like to be in the midst of such an historic metamorphosis? Moreover, there are not many places in the country where you'd have to go far afield to find a good man for such an assignment.

Another aspect of updating the Reformation, however, falls upon us Protestants. We must be able to give our people clear and competent reports about the achievements of Vatican II to date and a factual account of the issues under debate and decision during session four. The resources for this are abundant. You start with the conciliar decrees themselves: on the sacred liturgy, the Church and ecumenism (available as 25-cent pamphlets in any bookstore that stocks religious books). For reliable news coverage, general newspaper accounts are uneven and often uncomprehending. Our best sources are the Religious News Service and the News Service of the National Catholic Welfare Conference. Along with an updated account of the council, our people also need to know something of what the Roman Catholics are frankly calling their "new theology." The indignant Methodist layman who complained to me that "it is Catholic dogma that a man can save himself by good works and the merits of the saints," was healthily perplexed, if not wholly converted, to hear of Hans Küng's *Justification*, with its bold contention that the best of the Catholic tradition affirms and cherishes the *sola fide* (justification by faith alone). Protestants with a horror of formalism in worship or tyranny in church government should at least know about the first five volumes of *Concilium*—the 50-volume library which the "new breed" Catholic theologians are publishing as a crash program for the theological re-education of their people. Protestant stereotypes as to what Catholics are like can get even further knocked about if they will sample some of their current magazines and newspapers (*Jubilee, The Critic, The Catholic World, Commonweal*, for example)—some of them embrarrassingly better than our best.

But, again obviously, the most essential emphasis in Reformation Day, 1965 must be the challenge of church renewal for all Christians, today and tomorrow. We may speak more honestly of Luther's courage before the standing order of his day if we are willing to risk its equivalent in ours, of his recovery of the Gospel if we do ourselves still believe it, in our hearts. We are entitled to the thrills of "A Mighty Fortress . . . ," if we also feel a twinge of conscience at the passage, "let goods and kindred go, this mortal life also; the body they may kill . . ." The significance of our fathers' Reformation lies in its continuing challenge to us: what sort of reformation are *we* prepared for?

We ought to know by now that genuine church renewal comes from the reincarnation of the Gospel in faithful Christian witness and service in the world and not from pious griping and negative protests. We ought also to know—if history has any lesson to teach us—that authentic church renewal will never come from a resurgence of partisan denominationalism. Concern for church reform

and renewal must now and henceforth be genuinely ecumenical or it will be so much wishful thinking. This
means that Protestants and Catholics have now a common
stake, not merely in "brotherhood" and "spiritual fellowship," but in that unity in discipleship for which Jesus
prayed (John 17:21) —not that Christians might be cozy
but "that the world may believe."

There are, of course, those who'd rather fight than
switch. For them, the old patterns are still there to be repeated; and, as Jesus said of a similar group who were
blind to the signs of *their* times, "verily, they have their
reward." The rest of us, however, could well afford to
celebrate Reformation Day, 1965 by trying to get the
tortured history of Catholic-Protestant relationships into
new perspectives—by rejoicing with our Roman brethren
in their Reformation Roman-Style, by wishing them well
in their risks and opportunities of renewal, and by taking
thought as to how *we* may "go and do likewise," not for
ourselves only but for the world for which Christ died, in
which we, and *all* our Christian brethren, are set to witness and to serve.

CHAPTER 12

A BLOW FOR RELIGIOUS LIBERTY

September 29, 1965

A *Blow for Liberty* is the sequel to *Liberty Deferred*—but written some months later, in Rome on the night of September-ber 21, as a news story for *The All-Church Press,* a regional, Protestant religious news service [headquarters: Fort Worth] that supplies weekly parish newspapers for some 400 congregations across the nation. It appeared in their issue of September 29—as close to a scoop as a professional historian usually comes.

It is reprinted here because it tells how the explosion of the previous November 19 was followed up, in the opening days of session four, by a debate and vote that finally nailed the *Declaration on Religious Liberty* to the council's masthead. This was doubly important because it was *this* vote that set the tone and the pace for the session and assured its final triumphs.

I confess to an unwarranted pride in this story—for it amounts to a confirmation of a series of predictions I'd been making about the council's prospects since 1963. Earlier, my friends had made indulgent comments about the stars in Outler's eyes. Toward the end, they wondered how I had managed to make out so well. My secret: the discovery, almost in the beginning, that what the Secretariat for Promoting

Christian Unity really wanted, it always came close to getting, sooner or later. And I knew at firsthand and for certain that the Secretariat wanted a good *Declaration on Religious Liberty* as much as any of us observers. With such a reliable tip-off, my prognostications were not really as reckless as they may have seemed to some.

It has taken just eight days for session four of Vatican II to reach its first dramatic crisis and to register one of its most important victories. What was immediately at stake was the *Declaration on Religious Liberty*, but on this one issue hung the fate of the fourth session and the future of the progressive cause in the Roman Catholic Church. If the schema had been turned down, or if it had been stultified by a large negative vote, the still lurking suspicions of non-Catholics would have been revived and the old complaint that Catholics claim for themselves what they deny to others would have been renewed. Psychologically, at least, this question had become the test of sincerity of the council's profession of concern for open and honest dialogue with other Christians and with the rest of the world as well. Thus, today's thumping majority in favor of a clear affirmation of religious liberty (1,997 for to 224 against) was decisive in more ways than one. It has demonstrated what some of us had believed—and others doubted—that the Pope and the college of bishops are firmly committed to this crucial doctrine. It also has reduced the threat of further diehard obstructionist tactics and will help to hasten the council's final adjournment by mid-December, or even sooner.[1] Finally, it provided yet another striking instance of Pope Paul's courage and astuteness, for it was he who made the final decision that there should be a vote—thus holding the council to its own normal procedures and to his promise, made last

[1] Adjournment: December 8.

November, that there would be such a vote early in the fourth session. But this took courage, for he did this against entrenched resistance within the highest circles of the council management.

The session had opened (September 14) in an atmosphere of uneasiness and tension—partly because of the rumors that the diehards had regained some ground over the summer, partly because of the abrupt and unexpected appearance (September 11, just as the bishops were arriving in Rome) of a new papal encyclical, *Mysterium Fidei*, which bears the marks of a strong conservative influence in its reiteration of traditional Roman Catholic teaching about transubstantiation in the mass.

But this initial depression was quickly lifted by the Pope's address on the opening day in which he stressed the original Johannine theme of the council as an act of love toward all men—and then dropped the news, almost casually, that he was ready to establish the much discussed episcopal senate (*synodus episcoporum*) as a counterbalance to the Roman curia. The very next day he followed his words with action. When we met for the first general congregation, the Pope appeared in person to announce the actual plan and constitution of the synod. It was a memorable sight to see Paul VI walking quietly across the north transept of St. Peter's (instead of up the main east aisle)—without fuss or feathers. Then, after mass and the reading of the *motu proprio* establishing the synod, he walked back out again as unobtrusively as he had entered. The importance of the episcopal synod is that it will give more responsibility to the national and regional conferences of bishops than ever before. It is, therefore, a major step toward broadening the base of episcopal leadership in the Roman Catholic Church. If *Mysterium Fidei* had cheered the conservatives, this latest action pleased the progressives.

This done, the council moved briskly into the debate on

its first item of business: the *Declaration on Religious Liberty*. Everybody knew that this had already been twice debated and twice deferred, and that the diehards meant to block it again if they could. Everybody agreed that a majority of the bishops were for the declaration, but they disagreed as to how many others would vote a flat "no" in an actual balloting. The diehards claimed 600-675, which would have been enough to spoil the hope of moral consensus. The progressives were guessing that the "Noes" would number no more than 200 to 300 (the latter the number of negative amendments that had been turned into the Secretariat for Promoting Christian Unity). But nobody knew for sure—and that heightened the suspense.

It has been a gentle irony that every time this declaration had been deferred the next revision of the text turned out clearer and stronger than its predecessor. It is as if the *immobilisti* are forcing the council to go the limit in its assertion of religious liberty. The essence of the new text was the same as its predecessors: the Roman Catholic Church is prepared to go on record as affirming that no man may rightly be coerced into religious faith nor any man forcibly restrained from the conscientious expression of religious faith on any grounds save the just rights of other men in the same society! The plain fact is that this has not been traditional Catholic teaching since the days of Constantine. Thus the implications of a forthright *Declaration on Religious Liberty* (as distinguished from religious "toleration") cuts deeply into the nerve tissue of the old Roman mentality, with its accustomed claims to special privileges in "Catholic states," including civil suppression of non-Catholic worship.

From an ecumenical point of view, the declaration was crucial for serious further progress in the developing dialogue between Catholics and Protestants. As an American cardinal put it: "This is the test of our sincerity in the *Decree on Ecumenism*" (passed and promulgated November 21, 1964, which recognizes the validity of Christian baptism in Protestant Churches). In a real sense, therefore, the fate of the whole cause of *aggiornamento* was riding on this single issue.

As the debate progressed, two fixed positions emerged: all the Americans were for it and all but one of the nine Spaniards who spoke were against it. But the Italians, who had been in the opposition camp in the beginning, had now spread out across a whole range of positions—and it was an Italian bishop, Carlo Colombo (theological consultant to the Pope) who played the decisive role in the revision of the present text and in its being brought to a vote. Another impressive development was the nearly unanimous support that came from the bishops of dioceses in Communist countries. One of the high points of the debate came when old Cardinal Beran (Czechoslovakia) who has suffered grievously for his faith, first at the hands of the Nazis and then the Communists, arose to exhort his fellow bishops to strengthen, not weaken, this declaration. It is also significant because it was in the United States and in the Communist countries that Catholics first discovered the practical validity of a "free church" in a secular society.

In four and a half days 62 speakers from 29 different countries covered almost every conceivable aspect of the problem. The main argument of the diehards was twofold: this declaration forfeits the special privileges rightly due the Roman Catholic Church and is tantamount to an admission that other religions have equal rights with the true religion, at least in civil law. The progressive case was stated forcefully by an aged Belgian cardinal—ex-worker-priest—Joseph Cardijn: "In the light of 60 years of priestly experience, I solemnly affirm that a clear proclamation of civil liberty in matters religious is urgently necessary. . . . The Church can no longer act as in the Middle Ages, or colonial times. It must risk its entire case on the persuasive power of the Word of God which it proclaims, on its evangelical humility, on the truth of its doctrine."

The ratio of the 62 speakers for and against the declaration was about 6 to 3, and there are some 2,250 bishops in daily attendance in St. Peter's. The diehards insisted that the debate was representative, which would have suggested some 725 negative votes in a showdown— far too many for the declaration to be fully effective. The progressives devoutly believed that they had a large silent majority but they could not be certain. And so when the rumors began to fly that the coordinating commission was considering yet another deferral, there was widespread dismay—for this meant that the conservatives might then counterattack on other fronts as well and the council drag on and on. And it came very close to happening just that way. On Monday night, September 20, the coordinating commission met and voted against a vote in the council— but then, this morning (September 21) there was a vote on the declaration and it passed 1,997 to 224. What happened in between was a decisive act of Pope Paul's—directing that regular conciliar procedures be followed in this case as in others, and that his promise of a vote (made last November) be honored now. Last November he had supported the council management in going by the rules; now he overruled them when they proposed an exceptional procedure, insisting that now, as then, they go by the rules! In each instance, he was consistent and fair— first to the consternation of the progressives and then to the dismay of the diehards.

While the ballots on any given vote are being counted, the discussion in the *aula* (on other topics, mind you) goes on uninterruptedly. This time, the debate was on the famous Schema 13, *The Church in the Modern World*. This is obviously one of the most important documents on the council's agenda—but on this morning, the bishops were visibly distracted until the tally on vote 293 (*The Declaration on Religious Liberty*) was announced [*placet:* 1,997; *non-placet:* 224]. The minutes for the day record drily that "the proclamation of these results provoked widespread applause [forbidden by the rules!] through the hall, including the special tribune reserved for the observers." This was indeed the case!

And so came and passed one of the great moments in modern church history. The maximum mustered by the "triumphalists" in the real showdown was 224. And this makes it probable that they will not attempt another all-out obstruction of the progressive majority until we get to the schema on *The Relation of the Church to Non-Christian Religions,* where the crucial issue is a disavowal of anti-Semitism. It also means that before Christmas we shall have a conciliar declaration that will finally lay the ghost of Torquemada and snuff out "the light of burning martyrs."

Now the ecumenical dialogue can go forward in new terms of mutual trust and recognition between Protestants and Catholics, who are challenged on both sides to rearrange their respective prejudices against each other. Now, the rest of the council agenda will be handled with dispatch, for by this vote the bishops have set their course and calendar. Out of it all emerges the enigmatic figure of Paul VI with heightened stature—a man so unhappily misunderstood and underestimated by his Catholic and Protestant critics alike; a man who agonizes and hesitates and hears all sides in every crisis but who has regularly shown a firm, sure touch when the final move is called for.

It was a fascinating drama and a vital blow for liberty. But now the council connoisseurs are wondering: what can they do for an encore?

CHAPTER 13

POPE AND COUNCIL TURN A CORNER

October 8, 1965

Shortly after the preceding report for the Protestant papers I wrote another, similar piece for *The Oklahoma Courier,* but this one to Catholics and with an emphasis on what I had learned about the art of pope-watching as practiced in a conciliar crisis. Paul VI had first appeared as a man to reckon with in the closing days of session one when he and Cardinal Suenens had joined together to give the council a clear directive after the impasse of November ("The Suenens-Montini theses").[1] Then, after his election as Pope, one quickly grasped the obvious fact that he would be the human key to the labyrinth of the continuing council. I had been greatly impressed by his opening allocution to the second session, and in the ensuing months my confidence in the spirit and direction of his leadership had grown. But not without occasional moments of horrid doubt—for he is a highly complicated man and his determination to hold the incredible complexity of the Roman Catholic Church in balance and unity has frequent side-effects that are dismaying—now to one and now to another of the partisans of various causes.

What fascinated me most about him was the curious combination one saw of a "traditionalist" in doctrine and a

[1] See below, p. 178.

"progressive" in practical questions. Here, then, was a real conservative who was *not* an immobilist, and not a proxy for that party. Increasingly, I came to feel that this particular combination was providentially suited to the needs of the council and its aftermath.

I was, therefore, at least mildly disturbed by the mounting rash of criticism that sprang so effortlessly from people who had this grievance or that against the council or the curia or Italian politics, or—anything! Partisans of "the open Church" have a disconcerting way of blaming the *Pope* for not decreeing an open Church *by papal fiat*. Devotées of John XXIII found Paul VI an all too easy subject for invidious comparisons—ignoring the fact that Pope Paul was getting results that Pope John had failed to get with the conservatives. Worse than these mutterings was the outright malice of "Michael Serafian's" *The Pilgrim* (with its sensationalist revelations of Paul's betrayal of the council) and "F. E. Cartus" [same man] in the September, 1965 issue of *Harper's*—where Paul VI appears as Pio Nono *redivivus,* or worse.

My objection to these criticisms was twofold: they were wrong and they were mischievous. Their impact upon the council was bound to be unhelpful and I was also, perhaps needlessly, uneasy about their effect upon Paul VI, who was already moving as far beyond his own pre-conciliar boundary lines as one could reasonably expect—constantly exposed to pressures that gained extra strength from such miscues by the progressives.

It was scarcely *my* business to defend the *Pope* against *his* critics. But it went with my commitments to the council and its success to say a modest word of witness about an unusual man who was turning in an extraordinary performance in a refractory situation. The climax over the *Declaration on Religious Liberty* seemed a good time to say such a word, and a Catholic diocesan paper seemed a good place for it.

Pope-watching is an ancient art in Rome, as one can readily imagine—but now in the glare of the publicity focused on Vatican II, it has come to be a popular indoor sport with the non-Italian Catholics, the Protestant observers and, naturally, the journalists from all over. The image of the good Pope John is fortunately fixed in everyone's mind as the man whose vision opened the doors and windows of the Catholic Church to change, and whose boundless love warmed the whole world for the little while he was in the Chair of Peter. But the estimates of his successor, Paul VI, vary so widely as to baffle the conscientious historian. On one side, there are harsh and contemptuous appraisals of him, such as the one in a recent leading "literary magazine" in which a disenchanted (and discredited) Catholic priest has denounced him as a weakling obsessed with an archaic pride of office:

> Paul will allow no diminution of the almost flamboyant and certainly exaggerated adulation and reverence traditionally manifested to his office. On this point he is intransigent and unrelenting. He considers it a matter of life and death: Christianity depends on the maintenance of this. . . . He is a conservative man, fearful of change, suspicious of liberty. . . . He has refused the beckoning finger of history.

There are others, myself included, who find this sort of stuff false and foolish. We see in Paul a master statesman and tactician, as fully dedicated to *aggiornamento* as John ever was, and very much more aware of the risks and consequences—who has rescued the council from the stifling grip of the *immobilisti* into whose hands John XXIII had delivered it. John's vision of the council was indeed revolutionary, but his theology and methods were thoroughly old-fashioned. Paul VI is a very conservative theologian and a churchman whose prime passion is unity in the Church, but his personal style and practical methods are definitely more progressive than John's. He has naturally outraged the visionaries who had convinced themselves that the council was due to issue in the millennium; he has alarmed the diehards who have discovered a leader they cannot outmaneuver. Nevertheless, in just two years, he has managed to shift the council into high gear and to move a very large bloc of formerly moderately conservative bishops over to the moderately progressive side. This is obvious from any careful analysis of the mounting majorities in the successive tallies of the second and third sessions.

Now, in the first two weeks of session four, this same pattern of subtle, dialectical statecraft has been repeated in one of the most dramatic of the major crises in the council's history thus far. One remembers how, during the summer, reports of a mounting "curial backlash" and an increasing pressure by the reactionaries on the Pope began to fly about and multiply. There was, therefore, instant and widespread dismay among the progressives when, on the very eve of session four, the bishops were suddenly confronted with a major encyclical, *Mysterium Fidei,* which was all too obviously a reassertion of the traditional [since the Middle Ages] Roman teaching on the Eucharist. Here, plainly, was a reinforcement for the conservatives and a firm (almost heavy-handed) rejection of the rather slight flurry of new-fangled notions in sacramental theology that had begun to ferment in various quarters, notably Holland. Thus, the atmosphere at the opening session was noticeably glum. It began to brighten a bit when the Pope, in his address, went out of his way to emphasize the original Johannine theme of "universal love" in the Roman Catholic Church and from this Church to other Christians and all mankind—and when he added the announcement of his plan for an episcopal synod and his forthcoming peace-pilgrimage to the United Nations.

Most important of all was his follow-up the next morning with the actual directive that established the synod. We observers had the unusual privilege (because of our location) of being the first to be startled at the sight of the Pope walking into the council hall from the north transept of St. Peter's without a parade and to the visible consternation of his attendants (just two!). The day before we had watched him wave away the *sedia gestatoria* with a wry smile—as also last year we had watched him give away his Milanese tiara. Now, we saw him "assist" at a low mass in the *aula,* among his brother bishops, and then take his chair on the presidents' dais while the *motu proprio* establishing the synod was read out. That done, he got up and walked out as unobtrusively as he had come in, with a shy little wave to us as he passed by the observers' tribune. There is indeed an ancient cult of papal adulation in the Vatican, but the notion that Paul VI revels in it, or cultivates it, is arrant nonsense.

After this, the session moved quickly toward its first crisis because the very first item on the agenda was the hotly controverted, twice-deferred *Declaration on Religious Liberty.* Everybody knew that the only hope the opposition had for fending off this deadly threat to Roman triumphalism was by avoiding a decisive vote. Everybody also knew that a majority of the bishops were in favor of the declaration, but nobody was certain of its exact size. It was this uncertainty that gave the unfolding drama its unsettling suspense. If the majority was massive, the die-hards' whole cause was lost; if the minority was large enough (500 or more), the progressives (and the Pope) would be acutely embarrassed. Would we, or wouldn't we, find out where we stood? This was the question!

In the course of the debate, we heard 62 speakers from 29 different countries. The opposition advanced the traditional arguments: that religious liberty amounts to religious indifferentism; that it had already been condemned by former popes (Gregory XV and Pius IV); that it would forfeit the valid rights of Catholics to special privileges in "Catholic states." The superior-general of a major religious order (incidentally, a Frenchman) put the traditionalist case with blunt clarity: "Since the Catholic Church alone possesses the divine law and has the sole responsibility from God for teaching it, it alone has any real right to religious liberty. Other cults may be tolerated when they must be, but nothing should be done to encourage them."

The most impressive speech on the "progressive" side came from a Czech archbishop—himself a victim of religious persecution by both Nazis and Communists, who had just recently been released from prison:

> I affirm from experience that oppression of conscience is morally pernicious, even when it is intended or pretended to be on behalf of the true faith. Thus, the Church in my country now seems to be making painful expiation for the sins committed in the past against freedom of conscience in the name of the Church—for the burning of Jan Hus and the coercive reimposition of Catholicism on the Bohemian people. By such acts, the civil authorities, intending or pretending to serve the Church, actually wounded it. This trauma, lodged in the heart of my nation, has been an impediment to spiritual progress, and has given our enemies excuses for agitation. History is here urging us to declare the principle of religious freedom clearly and without any restrictions.

It is not without significance that it was Paul VI who had recently made this man (Josef Beran) a cardinal!

The proportion of affirmative and negative interventions in the 62 speeches on religious liberty was roughly 6 to 3. The diehards claimed that this was a representative ratio—which figured out to some 700 *non-placets* in an actual ballot. This would have been disastrous. The progressives claimed that there would be no more than 300—a prediction based on the number of negative *modi* (amendments) received by the Secretariat for Promoting Christian Unity since session three. But as the days passed and the substance of the debate wore thin, the question of a vote was still up in the air.

Everybody now knows what happened on Tuesday, September 21, but its significance needs still to be pondered. The moderators (appointed by Paul) divided 3 to

1 in favor of a vote; the coordinating commission (chiefly John's nominees) divided 14 to 12 against a vote. This would have settled the matter—for the time being. And then, overnight, Pope Paul overruled this decision and ordered a vote taken at the conclusion of the debate. Was this an arbitrary intervention by an absolute monarch? No—because the coordinating commission's decision to conclude this debate without a vote had itself been contrary to normal conciliar procedure. It should be remembered that last November, Pope Paul had sustained the council presidency in deferring a vote on a text that *had not been* fully debated at that time. Now he insisted on having a vote on a text that *had been* fully debated. In so doing, however, he ran the ticklish risk of being made to look bad at the U.N. if the *non-placets* ran above 300. The actual tally: Votes cast: 2,222; Yes: 1,997; No: 224; Null: 1.

The unofficial "minutes" of the day report somewhat drily: "The proclamation of these results provoked widespread applause throughout the hall, including the special tribune reserved for the observers." Why not—since this was in some ways the most decisive single moment in the council for us?

The Times of London was one of the few daily newspapers that immediately grasped the immense significance of this vote. In a lead editorial the next day, it pointed to the fact of the radical break with Catholic tradition and practice here represented—and went on to speak of "the debate on religious liberty and its outcome" as "a great event in the history of Catholicism and in the history of human liberty."

There are also important side-effects of this vote for the remainder of the council's program. For example, it settled the question as to whether the *immobilisti* have any further prospects of frustrating the progressive majority, and it made almost certain that the other schemas will be handled with dispatch at a high level of unanimity. The council will now surely be adjourned by mid-December or earlier. Moreover, the ecumenical dialogue can now go forward with renewed mutual confidence and trust—with more decisive pressure than ever before on the ancient prejudices that have hitherto hindered us from a real meeting.

And now also, perhaps, the snide suspicions of Pope Paul will begin to fade and his true quality be appreciated: this shy, intense, subtle man in the apostolic palace, galvanized by his zeal for church renewal, agonized by its risks and confusions, tortured by the grave decisions that are called for by a fantastically complicated situation, but acting swiftly and surely when the crises are finally matured. The visionaries and the rebels will go on being disenchanted because of the halting pace of the millennium. But they can be confidently ignored by the increasing number in the new crowd of pope-watchers who see in Paul's subtlety a much-needed match for the Byzantine intelligence of the *immobilisti*, in his political realism a caution and candor that commands respect, in his imagination (and courage to innovate) a motive force that may transform the Catholic Church more profoundly than any alternate pattern of leadership, given the present realities and the problems that loom beyond the council's close. Certainly, in these opening days of this concluding session of Vatican II, he has helped open the way into the future.

CHAPTER 14

REFORMATION ROMAN-STYLE

November 6, 1965

At the Paulist Fathers' reception for 1964, the speakers were Professor Warren Quanbeck (Lutheran World Federation) and Sister Mary Luke Tobin (Mother Superior of the Sisters of Loretto and an *auditrix* at the council). In 1965, I was invited a second time and gladly accepted since, with all the hospitality showered on us by the Paulists, anything they asked of us was a command performance.

The day was November 6—and it came at a more relaxed and mellow time than we had had in any session thus far. The great debates were over and the tensions of the council had shifted from St. Peter's to the commissions which were working frantically to prepare the necessary revisions of the remaining documents for the closing rush. Many of the bishops not on the commissions were having what amounted to a holiday since the general congregations were not meeting daily and even when they met the agenda was not very demanding. The only current crisis—which proved more curious than serious—had come when the Pope referred the question of updating the curial administration of indulgences to the review and comment of the various episcopal conferences. This was, one thought, a very good idea—a sort of experiment in collegiality on the spot, while the bishops were still together in Rome.

The results, however, were disconcerting. What they quickly discovered was that there were wide differences in the hierarchies in their understandings and interpretations of the theology of indulgences. Indeed, the whole problem area of repentance and penance was exposed in considerable disarray and it was quickly apparent that more careful theological reconsideration was needed than the circumstances then allowed. The project was quietly withdrawn but not before the confusion had become mildly embarrassing.

In the main, however, the prospects of the council's ending on a high note were cheerful and firm. It was now time to look beyond to the exciting epoch looming up as aftermath. It seemed to me also a time to look back over the road we'd come—so far in four short years!—and once again to try for a perspective on the unlikely and momentous reformation that had been wrought.

Eminences, excellencies, fathers and brethren—and sisters—in Christ:

Let me say directly, simply and sincerely that I greatly appreciate this honor of speaking to you, yet once again, on this happy occasion of the Paulist Fathers' reception. Each year, it has been one of the most gracious gatherings of the session, and our contacts and acquaintances formed or extended here have been greatly meaningful in our experience of the council. We observers are, therefore, doubly indebted: to the Paulist Fathers for their hospitality and unstinted devotion to the ecumenical enterprise, and to the American hierarchy and their *periti* for their countless courtesies and their zealous tuition of us in the ways and mazes of the Roman Catholic Church in council.

It has been said that there are four "parties" among the bishops, *periti* and Catholic journalists: diehards, conservatives, progressives, and arsonists. *Mutatis mutandis,* one might speak of four "types" among the observers and onlookers: "Hussites," skeptics, admirers and visionaries. The "Hussites" believe that there is still time for you to revoke our safe-conduct passes and to close the council with an auto-da-fé in the Piazza di Sant'Uffizio. The skeptics see many outward signs of change but, knowing Rome of old, they regard these as illusions. The admirers readily admit that great things have been wrought here in council, but they fear that once the tumult and shouting are over, the tide of reform will ebb away, leaving only your noise-makers clamoring for what might have been. The visionaries, however, believe that you really have let the ecumenical genie out of the bottle, that you have opened Pandora's box of trouble and hope—if ever so slightly on some points—and thus have committed yourselves to at least a generation of exacting, exciting and rewarding work, trying to bring the Church's thought and practice up to the level of the council's vision. By "Hussite" charge and my own frank admission, I belong among the visionaries—and it is in this spirit that I speak to you today.

Now is the time for all good men to turn in their appraisals of Vatican II—and to try to keep from treading on each other's platitudes. Here we are, virtually at the end of the most epochal event in modern church history, already in the initial stages of the new era, on the verge of the enormous undertakings (and confusions) of the post-conciliar period. Each of us has to put all this in some sort of perspective, if only to place himself in the new situation and its involvements.

And yet, just as inevitably, our best efforts at appraisals are bound to be inadequate, for at least two reasons. One is the sheer scope of the council—far too many blind men reporting their impressions of much too large an elephant. Our other bafflement, more subtle and tantalizing, is that every appraisal is already preshrunk along the bias of one's *expectations* of the council, one's calculations of the gap between its *possibilities* (at this stage or that) and its *performance* (on this point or the other). There are, as we know, those with a fine show of prophetic fervor, who complain that the council has not ushered in the millennium, that it has not really met all the needs of a desperate world, that it has not actually accomplished the reunion of all Christians. This means, of course, that their expectations were formed of the dream-stuff that sells hair tonic.

There are others who complain, with a curious mixture of bitterness and pathos, that the council has dared to tamper with ancient ways and notions, ratified by papal teaching and sanctified by curial administration. Obviously, their expectation of the council was that it should have confirmed the status quo.

There are those who complain that the council has been too "churchy," too much preoccupied with ecclesiastical housekeeping, not radically involved in the exigencies and agonies of the world that huddles under the walls of the Leonine City and that stretches to the Pentagon, the Kremlin and the jungles of Vietnam. There are those who fear another Protestant reformation and yet others who seem to think that one is overdue—as the priest who, at one point in this curious affair of the indulgences, asked me if I knew where there was a handy bulletin board where he could tack up another round of theses for debate.

My own prime bias in this matter is historical. Thus, I keep on being astonished at how far you have come from where you started and am still puzzled as to just how you made it. But I am certain that there is no hope at all of rightly estimating the achievements of Vatican II if you skimp its prehistory: the successive humiliations of the papacy, first by devoutly Christian monarchs, and thereafter by the two Napoleons and the secular liberals; the successive crises of revolution and anti-clericalism that turned the Vatican into a beleaguered fortress, fortified by the firm conviction that the world of *those* times was irreconcilably antipathetic; the successive alienations of the European intelligentsia and the workers; the stubborn maintenance of the old church-state theories even while Roman Catholics in North America and the missions were discovering that they could do very well without them; the two centuries of what E. E. Y. Hales has called "that long sequence of censures [of the world] codified by Pius IX, given a philosophical basis by Leo XIII, supplied with teeth by St. Pius X and sublimated by Pius XII." It was *this* prehistory that set the stance and policies of the Roman Catholic Church, right up to the eve of the council. This is why the initial odds were so slight that what has happened could have happened. For one remembers that the early preparations for the council were made inside the beleaguered fortress by its chief defenders. The first schemas, in the summer of 1962, were plainly dominated by their siege mentality.

It was, of course, the genius of Pope John XXIII that transformed this mood and mind-set, that flung the Catholic Church into the maelstrom of the *modern* world with an optimism born of an invincible goodness that even cynics were abashed by, and with a breathtaking, simplehearted confidence that the Church would fare better in free encounter with men of goodwill, that Christian unity might become a live option if Rome were renovated. It was this charismatic vision, this heartlifting demonstration of the irresistible power of Christian graciousness, that brought the council into being and gave it its distinctive character. It is in this sense that Vatican II is and always will be Pope John's council.

But the fact is that its first session settled nothing, really—except that the council had to be continued. It has been the genius of Pope Paul, and others who with him had grasped the substance of the Johannine vision, to guide the council through the complex maze it has threaded from the confused gropings of session one to the now nearly humdrum consensus of session four. The pattern of this leadership is far too complex to summarize here and naturally I see it through a glass darkly. But, on any accounting, it has been an extraordinary performance and one, I think, that is still greatly underestimated.

One of the most striking impressions of these four years is that this council has regularly failed to follow its script —none of the several that have been in readiness from time to time. Plainly, it has not turned out quite as Pope John envisaged it; it is certainly not the council that the ante-preparatory commissions prepared for. It has not filled the prescriptions of the *immobilisti*—and yet the progressives can hardly claim that they have called the tune for every stave. The most advanced of its documents bear visible traces of *piononismo;* even the most conservative reflect something of the spirit of *aggiornamento*.

It goes with the epoch-making character of Vatican II that it has been a council chiefly of *charters:* of new beginnings and mandates. Far less has been accomplished than has been made possible. More frontiers have been opened up than occupied. As vast as the agenda has been, it is slight in comparison with the budget of unfinished business you have produced—for yourselves, your priests, your scholars (lay and clerical) your lay folk and, not least of all, for us separated brethren who must now find appropriate ways to reciprocate. The real meaning of most of the conciliar documents has still to be worked out in practice—in the Church in the modern world. For example, the keystone of the *Constitution on the Church* is collegiality, but what does it mean? What the text seems to say, what the *nota explicativa* seems to imply or something else again? Nobody knows, nor will we until we have watched it at work over a sizable span of years, in a trial-and-error process, the first ambiguous sequences of which have already taken place. If the *collegium episcoporum* ever really gets the hang of acting collegially, the resultant doctrine will look hopeful. If not, the charter

of the *Constitution on the Church* will fall into de-
suetude. And so it will be with all the other conciliar documents that have broken new ground: ecumenism,
religious liberty, Christian-non-Christian relations, etc.
Their real meaning has yet to be determined by their
translation into the basic experiences and understandings
of the People of God. Then we shall know how much is
substance and how much was conciliar rhetoric.

But the most truly unique aspect of *this* council lies in
its deliberate concern for reform within the limits of
Christian community and in vital continuity with the
Christian past. Vatican II has been as self-consciously a
reforming council as Constance was, or Florence, or
Trent—but with a decisive difference. Usually, reformers value truth above community and, having the truth,
they will ruthlessly sacrifice community—with pious re-
luctance (as at Augsburg) or with pious exuberance (as
with the anathemas of Trent). Standard operating procedure for other reforming councils has been to separate
the sheep from the goats and then to scape the goats and
fit out the sheep with halos. Vatican II is a very rare instance of historic change within a continuum of identity
and consensus. One cannot miss the evident concern here
for reform without schism in the soul of the Church—in
the face of intransigence that has sometimes seemed to
reach over and beyond the call of duty. This is what I
mean by my corny title, Reformation Roman-Style. Vatican II has been a council that has dismayed the diehards
but has not alienated them, that has damped down the
arsonists without quenching their fire, that has chafed
the progressives and bored the unimaginative. It has been
a subtle affair, in which some of the changes are only
"developments" and some of the "developments" are real
changes; where much is left open to further development and/or change—and where an adequate theory for
this particular kind of development and/or change has

yet to be developed. In my judgment, this is one of the most interesting of all the problems generated by this council. It opens up a whole cluster of theoretical and practical problems, all bearing on the vital ecumenical question of *the role of the Church in history* and *the role of history in the Church.*

This distinctive style of reformation has not been without design. Pope John's notion of *aggiornamento* was meant to imply reform and has done so—though not in the classical styles of Hus, Gerson or Savonarola. In accepting and modulating the Johannine program, Pope Paul has become the highly reflective director of an incredibly complex enterprise that is solidly conservative in doctrine and discipline, on the one hand, and vigorously progressive in polity and program, on the other. He will have no tampering with the core of traditional doctrine; yet he has already initiated more changes in traditional papal polity and practice than any Pope since Pius IX. There are, however, many changes initiated by Vatican II that may not touch the core of essential doctrine, but that do pose tricky problems for the tradition of invariable traditions. The *immobilisti* have often been quite right when they have complained that the new formulations of collegiality, ecumenism, religious liberty and Christian-Jewish relations have altered traditional patterns of teaching that run back for centuries. They have been wrong only in their *non sequitur* that these formulations are improper *because* they entail significant change. Thus, one of the important consequences of your Reformation Roman-Style is that in it you have continued to maintain a stable community in terms of unstable theories about that stability and these theories now require re-examination. This, too, is an item in your budget of unfinished business.

The main thing, however, is that thus far you have avoided many of the standard ways of mismanaging reformations. One of these has been to strike down dissent and to damn the heretics, in the name of some *proprietary system* of truth. Another: to bulldoze the conscientious minority (especially if it is more proud than pitiful!). A third: to rend the bonds of Christian community in the name of one version of the Gospel or in some perfectionist protest against the imperfect structures of the visible Church. A fourth way is for timid reformers (and more reformers are more timid than they appear or will admit) to give up after their first manhandling by "the ecclesiastical housekeepers."

But Reformation Roman-Style would seem to have its pitfalls, too. The most obvious is the illusion that a reform well-launched is somehow guaranteed a successful voyage. But it is all too plain that reforms and reformers are normally better in the sprints than in the marathon—that liberals have a distressing tendency to quit too easily or to count their chickens in the incubator. One wonders and worries about the swiftly ebbing tide of the reform spirit in this council in these last days. Something like this was due, but it has come sooner and is more drastic than I expected. The consequences of this can be serious, now that the real work of actualizing the council in the Church and the world is just beginning.

The other danger, also clear and present, is the excess of the special virtue of this sort of reformation. In your laudable preference for community above polemics—for progress without schism—will you settle for anything less than your own highest possibilities? In your realistic concern to bring everybody along together, will you be careful not to hobble those who run on ahead—some of whom are your ablest and choicest spirits? The good *is* the enemy of the best and we have already had that spelled out in more ways than one in these last days. One of the strongest impressions I have gained here is of an enormous pool of talent and an immense capital fund

of expectant zeal—in your *periti,* priests and people—
and I can't help hoping and praying that you will find
ways and the will to turn this huge potential loose on the
world (and in the world) in patterns that are somewhat
more apostolically radical than the essentially genteel
and civilized essays of Vatican II. God knows we Protestants have no shining alternatives to cite, no Archimedean
standpoint from which to press a longer lever than yours.
But in a world literally perishing for redemptive love,
we all have need of mutual exhortation. Each has the
right to rejoice at *all* the charisms of the Spirit—now so
abundant in *your* midst—and to hope for their fullest
fruition for the good of the entire Christian community.

There will be no more meetings of this sort again in
our lifetime. Our ways from here lie in a thousand directions—all in God's keeping, thank God! The splendors of
Vatican II—this strange interlude when we have been
so strangely one—will fade and be filed in the archives of
our memories. But a new advent of the Holy Spirit has
happened in our world in our time—an epiphany of love
that has stirred men's hearts wherever they have glimpsed
it incarnated. We saw that ourselves in the extraordinary
uprush of faith and hope in the city of cynics when Pope
Paul visited New York. In lesser ways, is not this task of
incarnating the spirit of Vatican II a possibility and imperative for us all as the council goes into its diaspora?

What must not fade is the clear conviction set down in
the *Decree on Ecumenism* that "there can be no ecumenism worthy of the name [nor any effective outreach to
the world] without interior conversion . . . , a change
of heart and holiness of life." The way to Christian unity
is long and arduous—and the end is not in sight. But on
such a way, as on all other providential journeys, the pilgrim People of God walk by faith and not by sight. Pope
Paul has wisely warned us against a facile hope and a false
irenicism that trifles with the grave issues that have so

long divided us. But even this warning is full of hope and is itself a landmark on our way.

Meanwhile, the least we can do is to remember that our confidence is not in ourselves, that our vocations are not for ourselves and cannot be exercised by ourselves. We are Christ's, and our mission is in and for the world for which Christ died. That mysterious high moment in the mass—*per ipsum et cum ipso et in ipso* (by Christ and with Christ and in Christ)—calls us to attention by its solemn reiteration of the basic formula for the apostolate of the whole People of God. This, at least, is what I have come to believe is the deepest level of the truth we confess *together* in that familiar refrain that you—and now we—seem to sing with more fervor than any other of your hymns:

Christus vincit, Christus regnat, Christus, Christus imperat!

CHAPTER 15

CHARTERS FOR CHANGE

January 26, 1966

The necessary time and money for the job of being an observer for the full duration of the council were generously provided me by my university over and beyond the call of its duty. As grateful part-payment of this "debt" I had done several reports to various groups on campus and had written two articles for our alumni magazine, *The Perkins Journal*. After session four, it seemed appropriate to attempt a "final report" to the university and community, in a public lecture. That lecture is included here as a sort of rounding out of my account of the council, from eve to adjournment—with a look ahead but also with inevitable echoes and repetitions from earlier statements.

Seven weeks after its adjournment, we were in mid-passage from the excitements of the council as accomplished fact to the sobering challenges of its long-range aftermath. The most important point that needed making then—and still—is that Vatican II opened new and unexpected frontiers for renewal and dialogue but *we* have to cross over and settle them. What the conciliar "charters for change" really signify is just beginning to be understood and realized by Roman Catholics. What they mean as challenges to and opportunities for Protestants and Orthodox has scarcely yet come clear even to the most concerned and clairvoyant. I spoke of this as responsibly as I could, at the time, but it will take the years ahead to decide what I should have seen and said.

Vatican II is over. Its 16 documents are now part and parcel of official Roman Catholic teaching. As long as the council was in process, there were open questions on many controverted points, always the chance of further turns and twists in the complex conflict between the various tendencies of the bishops. There was also that special excitement that goes with history-in-the-making and this held to the very end.

But Vatican II belongs now to history, and the new era it inaugurated has begun. What comes next is, therefore, aftermath—and it, too, will have its own excitements. For if the conciliar texts are fixed, their actual significance in practice must now be demonstrated in the upcoming future. As always, the promulgation of its documents is only half the story of a council. Its other half depends upon their reception. What will the Roman Catholic Church make of its council now? What will the rest of Christendom make of it? And what about the rest of the human community?

Already, the estimates of it vary so widely that it is hard to tell that they are actually estimates of the same event. There was, for example, a letter to *The Oklahoma Courier* last week which said bluntly that the council was a flat failure:

> Vatican II substituted a new set of rules for an old set concerning trivia. It settled to satisfy (sic!) the complacent self-righteous Catholic. It did little for man's suffering from too many births, too little food, too much ignorance, too inhuman a way of worship. Vatican II was a failure.
>
> /s/ Disappointed Catholic

And then there was the letter I received from a New Jersey Protestant named Ambrose Johnson:

> It is an absolute fact that the Roman Catholic Church is positively operating chiefly tactical (sic!), with the express intention of putting Protestants and non-Roman Catholics off their guard. . . . It is the crystal-clear intention of the Roman Church to have unification of Christians by surrender and absorption—for all Protestants to bring their wealth and assets over to the Roman Church to swell their present fabulously wealthy coffers and to extend their devastating power over all peoples of the world.

Over against this one places the agreed testimony of really responsible and competent Protestant observers— e.g., Professors Robert McAfee Brown, K. E. Skydsgaard, Dean Robert E. Cushman, *et al.*—who saw the council at work and up close and who have adjudged it as an unprecedented act of self-examination and reform: a Church turning away from its traditional triumphalism toward a more deeply biblical understanding of itself as the community of the People of God, a Church really eager to offer itself to the world in witness and service.

There are, as we all know by now, the Catholic diehards like Father Gomar De Pauw, of the Catholic Traditionalist Society—whom I got to know slightly last fall and found surprisingly like some of the *Protestant* housewreckers I have known. He does not reject the conciliar decrees outright; that would put him beyond the pale. Instead, he has convinced himself that they are most validly interpreted according to his own traditionalist views, in sharp contrast to the deplorable "Protestantizing tendencies" of the conciliar progressives. Meanwhile, he continues his fantastic game of peekaboo with Cardinal Shehan and Bishop Faveri (excardination, incardination and all that) which may very well get him into trouble.

Against this, we would have to set the faintly condescending approval of De Pauw's antithesis—Professor Hans Küng—in last week's *Commonweal:*

> The council has certainly not done everything which it could have done from the point of view of the present situation, but it has done a great deal more than we expected earlier. . . . Despite real disillusionment, the council has been the fulfillment of a great hope.

Incidentally, when I left Rome, there was a story going around that Cardinal Ottaviani had died and had not checked in at either purgatory or heaven. Since heaven was pleased with the cardinal's performance toward the end of the council, a search party was sent to retrieve him. They found him easily enough, up to his ears in boiling pitch but with a fiercely triumphant gleam in his one good eye. "Your Eminence," said the leader of the rescue squad. "there's been a great mistake. You are not supposed to be *here.* We've come to take you straight to heaven."

"Many thanks," said the cardinal shaking his head, "but what you can't see is that I'm standing on the shoulders of Hans Küng and I'm not moving until this stuff freezes over!"

Meanwhile, the shape of the post-conciliar era begins to emerge. Two weeks ago, Pope Paul designated the coordinating commission which will supervise the implementation of the Vatican decrees. Its composition is fair warning that the conservative-progressive tension will continue. The conservatives and the progressives are neatly balanced—and the key figure turns out to be the council's secretary general, Uncle Pericles Felici (who will inevitably get his red hat at the next consistory). At the same time, however, the Secretariat for Promoting Christian Unity—the strongest and most effective champion of the progressive cause in Rome—has been given *permanent* status. Moreover, a new Institute for Advanced Studies in

Ecumenism is being projected for Jerusalem—directed by an autonomous Academic Council, in which the Roman Catholics are by their own motion a minority without veto. If this experiment works—if it gains financial support from private sources so that it will not have to depend on church subventions—it will be one of the really crucial spearhead operations in the post-conciliar period. Any day now, we may hear of a batch of new cardinals, and before Easter the Pope is expected to announce the convocation of the first synod of bishops—a major new departure in representative policy-making at the summit. The terms and the agenda of this first session of the synod will be eagerly studied as a clue to the practical meaning of the theory of collegiality, at least in the first phase of the council's aftermath.

All of this is to say that the real meaning of Vatican II is still by way of being unfolded. The council changed the atmosphere within the Roman Church and between the several Churches—and it stirred the interest and hopes of a multitude of men. But it must finally be judged in terms of its formal commitments—its 16 charters for change—and by their implementation in the life and ethos of the Roman Catholic Church.

We Protestants are so accustomed to breaches with the past—we often call them *"progress"*—that we find it difficult to appreciate how complex and unsettling the problem of change is for men who are deeply immersed in their historical heritages and who cherish their links with the living past. We must, therefore, make a real effort to realize how sudden changes in ancient and solid traditions raise for Catholics the ghost of error in the Church. If the past can be so readily corrected or surpassed, how does one down the doubt that present traditions may have lurking errors in them that may have to be corrected by later generations who become aware of them? But what does this do to the theory of a perfect and wholly reliable deposit of the whole Christian system in the one true Church? To be sure, one can allow for changes that are no more than the filling out of partially developed truths. But changes that alter or correct a long standing tradition of teaching are bound to generate chain reactions of anxiety with respect to the teaching authority of the infallible Church.

Vatican II differed from previous councils chiefly in its predominantly *pastoral concern*—and this by design. Pope John made it quite clear that he wanted no new dogmas pronounced, no old anathemas reheated. Pope Paul VI has continued in this vein. But even the most common-place pastoral problems root back in doctrinal and moral reflections. Men cannot speak as pastors (neither to their own flocks nor to others "not of this fold") without appropriate theoretical reconsiderations. The updating of pastoral concerns and perspectives at Vatican II was bound to entail the updating of Catholic doctrinal and moral notions. This, in turn, was bound to produce mutations which can be called "developments" only by stretching that word past the limits of clear and distinct ideas.

It was on *this point,* more than any other, that the conflicts of the council turned. The immobilists were quick to spot any new idea in a given text (even if it was only an ancient one revived!) and they were as quick to raise the cry of "innovation." The progressives were just as quick to deny the charge of innovation, arguing that what seemed new was really older than the recent traditions which only seemed old to those who had never known anything better.

But the fact is that some of the "developments" of Vatican II amount to substantive modifications of long standing traditions of official teaching and practice. On this point the diehards were dead right. But it was precisely *these* "developments"—which sooner or later might just as well be called *changes* and so be done with playing coy!—it was, I say, just these *changes* that constituted the genius of Vatican II. *They* are the forward thrusts that have set the important agenda for the post-conciliar era. There are, therefore, two ways in which the achievements of Vatican II can still be stultified. One would be their nullification on purpose, or by neglect. The other would be a failure to provide an adequate theory of change in the Church to validate the dynamisms that Vatican II has set in motion, so as to allow for their continuing and cumulative action in the future—in short, what the Reformers had in mind with their phrase *semper reformanda* (a *permanent process* of development). It seems to me, therefore, that one of the best ways to understand Vatican II, both as a past event and as a source for the creative confusions still to come, is to focus on these items of significant change and to ponder their import for the future.

When the council began (October 8, 1962), it had a sprawling agenda of 73 schemas, in varying stages of immaturity. The first session saw nothing finished. But toward its close (December 4) Cardinals Suenens and Montini (prompted by Pope John) proposed a focus for all of the issues before the council, in terms of three correlated questions to be answered by the bishops: What does the Roman Catholic Church have to say to itself about itself? What does it have to say to the other Christians about the unity of the Christian community? What does it have to say to the world about righteousness, peace and human welfare? [1]

With this program as a guide, the 73 schemas were then regrouped and reduced to 13, and then rearranged in a cluster of 16, the final number. One of these is an ordinary constitution (*The Sacred Liturgy*); two are "dogmatic" constitutions (*The Church* and *Divine Revelation*); one is called a "pastoral" constitution (*The Church in the Modern World*). Besides these there are nine decrees and

[1] See above, p. 153.

three conciliar declarations. Most of these, naturally enough, deal with the Roman Catholic Church's *self*-understanding—the Church at worship, the Church in its essence, order and mission, the ground of its authority, its pastoral government, etc., etc., etc. One of the decrees [on ecumenism] and one of the declarations [religious liberty] deal specifically with the Roman Catholic Church's approach to the other Christian Churches—as do important sections of the *Constitution on the Church* and the *Decree on the Church's Missionary Activity*. The result: the re-opening of an ecumenical dialogue between Rome and the rest of Christendom after centuries of sullen silence, punctuated by growls. In the *Declaration on Religious Liberty*, the *Constitution on the Church in the Modern World*, and the *Declaration on the Relationship of the Church to Non-Christian Religions* the council speaks a loving word to all men of goodwill in the name of human dignity and authentic Christian community.

All of these documents reflect one degree or another of development in the sense of an extension or refinement of existing tradition. By the same token, all of them speak out of a profound awareness of Catholic tradition. But there are at least seven points in them where I think I see significant *change* in the sense of *actual alteration* from what has been official and standard. I list them in passing for there's no time to argue the evidence for my thesis that they are genuine mutations.

1. The most obvious "change," in the *Constitution on the Sacred Liturgy*, is the switch from Latin to the vernacular. It may be argued, and rightly, that this is merely the restoration of ancient tradition but, given the constancy of the Latin mass for seven or eight centuries, this switch to the vernacular is at least a vivid *psychological* change—as one can see from the hubbub it has caused. Far deeper here, however, is the change in the basic understanding of liturgy—from an essentially private affair of

congregated individuals to the notion of the sacramental miracle that transforms a group of alienated people (alienated from God, from themselves and from each other) into a band of brothers, in meaningful communion with God and the neighbor. Here *is* significant change from the post-Tridentine tradition of private worship and a charter for further mutations in sacramental theology.

2. Again, there is in the *Constitution on the Church* the compound notion of the Church as mystery (therefore beyond all sovereignty), as the People of God (therefore a general priesthood with a universal call to witness and holy living) and the Church as governed not simply by the bishop of Rome but by the entire *college* of bishops (therefore representative and local). Such a conception of the Church, in this form, has no precedent in the history of Christian doctrine, but it is bound to have far-reaching consequences, not yet fully foreseeable.

3. The *Decree on Ecumenism* marks a decisive change from both popular Catholic belief and official papal teaching (e.g., *Mortalium Animos*, 1928). Here, then, is a new perspective that promises to alter the relationships between the Roman Catholic Church and the other Christian churches. The *Decree on Ecumenism* is not a charter for church unity negotiations—this will come later —but it is a milestone from which further progress can be measured, and guided.

4. There was never any doubt that the *Declaration on Religious Liberty* was the test case for the progressive cause in the council. It was fought over for four years; it is the most carefully drafted of all the 16 documents—and, in the end, it polled 70 negative votes out of 2,300 plus. The immobilists insisted that its teaching is contrary to Scripture, tradition and explicit papal teaching—and they were right as far as the tradition since Augustine is concerned and explicit papal teaching since Gregory XVI. What is at stake in this instance is not merely the con-

demnation of religious persecution. Actually, what matters is the far-reaching theological implication of the recognition that rival claims to Christian truth must be settled in a fair forum in an open society. Over *there* is the ancient Scylla of *dogmatism*. Over *here* is the Charybdis of *religious indifferentism*. The *Declaration on Religious Liberty* is meant to be charter and chart for navigating the tricky passage in between.

5. The *Declaration on the Relationship of the Church to Non-Christian Religions* represents yet another real change—the happy outcome of another bitter conflict (recounted in an inaccurate and misleading article in a recent issue of *Look*). In addition to the vicious political propaganda that swirled about it, there was the immobilist charge that it was a departure from tradition (as it was!) and, therefore, unwarranted (as it wasn't!). Of all the crises in the council, this got closest to the marrow of sheer prejudice. In the showdown, there was no prudent option left open and the bishops *had* to vote their consciences. And yet, the affirmative majority topped 93 percent. Incidentally, the dropping of the word "deicide" from the text was *not* a weakening of the statement. It had become a "shibboleth" to partisans on both sides, thus, dangerously equivocal. What the decree does is to describe anti-Semitism in action and to condemn it unequivocally.

6. Two more important instances of the mutation of traditional teaching appear in the pastoral *Constitution on the Church in the Modern World*. That constitution itself was an unprecedented experiment in trying to formulate and communicate the Roman Catholic Church's understanding of and concern for her secular environment. The result is not a masterwork in Christian social ethics but it is a landmark in the Roman Catholic Church's involvement in man's hungers and hopes in a world in agony. And, in the section on war and peace, there is a virtual abandonment of the medieval doctrine of the just war in

favor of a moderate pacifism neither doctrinaire nor yet quite utopian. The new theory has the same intent as the old but the shift is great enough to prompt reconsideration of a good deal of conventional teaching in this area since the Crusades.

7. In the section on marriage and the family there is what may very well amount to a drastic change in the traditional teaching of the Latin Church since Augustine, on the primary end(s) of conjugal love. Cardinal Ruffini —who made 30 speeches in the council in four years, all in opposition!—went to some lengths to make the point that, since Augustine, the Church has taught consistently that sex has only *one* legitimate end: procreation. This is the fundamental objection to *any* sort of contraception. Here we come finally to the most important of all the *unresolved* issues of Vatican II—birth control—which some of us also think of as its greatest failure. What they were looking for was an ideal or perfect solution and they couldn't find it—and so chose to stand by their old tradition, *ad interim.* But what they also did was to recognize that there are compound aims and values in love and marriage—procreation *and* interpersonal communion—both primary but not identical. This opens the way to further reconsideration of the question and provides a charter for the changes that are bound to come sooner or later—perhaps when medicine comes at the problem from the angle of precisely *timed* ovulation instead of *an*ovulation, which would allow for conception consciously intended instead of consciously intended *contra*ception.

No one yet knows for certain how these Vatican charters will be translated into action and how far they will move the Roman Catholic Church to further changes—and what impact all this will have on the Christian community as a whole and on the human community. The council itself captured the public imagination as no other event in the church history of this century. But who will follow it up, and how, and how far?

The first factor in the follow up will be getting the documents read and interpreted and their essential imperatives communicated to as many people as possible, in the Roman Church and out of it. In this connection, they will at least have easy access to the primary sources. Most of them have already been published in the diocesan papers. They are, or shortly will be, available in separate pamphlets and, in late March, the whole lot will be published in a single volume together with Catholic and Protestant commentaries. Similar publishing programs are in progress in other countries all over the world. In many dioceses here in America, plans are afoot for "little councils": to repeat something of the experience of the council for the priests and people back home. Even so, this business of getting the council to the people will have to go on in a thousand ways and for a generation; nor will it really succeed until it gets to the community and parish levels, with study and service projects—e.g., "living room dialogues"—in which Catholics and non-Catholics can learn to think, work and worship together in mutual trust.

Another crucial factor in the post-conciliar follow up will be the leadership patterns of the Pope. The art of pope-watching, a perennial fascination in Rome, has now become an important interest for any and all ecumenists. I offer you here a thumbnail sketch, mostly to suggest our need for an accurate life-size portrait. It was, of course, John XXIII who begat the council, but it was Paul VI who carried it through to a success it could scarcely have had otherwise—and this because Paul is a deep-dyed conservative in matters of doctrine and church discipline yet also an imaginative and courageous progressive in questions of polity and administration. His passion for solidarity tempers his zeal for progress, but does not quench it. He is not indecisive, as has been alleged. What happens is that, with a darting intelligence, he canvasses all of the options in an issue, and all their competing claims. But then when he finally comes to the decision, it usually has an accent of inspiration—something original and un-expected—which means that we almost always have something more than the resultant of the merciless pressures that zero in on the fourth floor of the apostolic palace. He is tender with the feelings of the immobilists but declines to give them the veto power that they really want. His trusted lieutenants still come from the conservative side (Cicognani, Tisserant and Felici—who now becomes the man to watch, for he is the youngest man in the conservative leadership and his star has been rising) . But this same Pope has also begun internationalizing the College of Cardinals, has set up the synod of bishops and has partici-pated in a service of common prayer with the observers, despite *very strong dissuasion.* He exasperates those who want Rome reformed by Friday; he annoys the journalists who work on the "Let's you and them fight!" principle. And, alas, he simply does not enchant people, as Pope John did so effortlessly.

There are immobilists and progressives who join in pre-dicting that Pope Paul will try to turn the clock back from the hours that were struck in Vatican II. There is an Ar-gentine archbishop, whom I know slightly (Buteler of Mendoza) , who has said openly that Paul let the council go through with its playacting at reform, but now will qui-etly set things back to rights, just as they were *before Ron-calli!* This, of course, is nonsense. But we *can* expect him to go on in the pattern of cautious reform that he has al-ready displayed—open to new ideas or new dimensions of old ideas but immune from extremism.

And, he will also go on "developing"—himself! For example, when Vatican II began, Montini's concept of ecumenism was modelled on *Mortalium Animos*; his stereotype of Protestantism was borrowed from the only really bad book Jacques Maritain ever wrote (Montini translated it into Italian). In the course of the council, however, his ecumenical understanding has developed as far and as fast as anyone's I know. His dealings with the observers went far beyond the demands of his Italian hospitality (which was superb) and of his Christian graciousness (which was unfailing). He still insists on a visible symbol and agency of unity in the Christian community and he regards the papacy as the only possible symbol and agency of this. But he now affirms that authentic unity need be neither monolithic nor uniformitarian—which means that he has come to take pluralism seriously and to react toward it positively.

Given such a perspective—and a decade of development —the shape of the eventual recomposition of Christian unity may become visible: a plurality of Churches in full communion, with diverse rites and institutional organization, but truly one in Christ as one Church but multiform —truly catholic, evangelical and reformed (to quote the slogan of COCU!). There is no *immediate* prospect of this; all of us need more growing up and growing together before we are ready for the risks of reunion. Meanwhile, however, we can get on with the obvious and urgent projects of mutual Christian witness and service in joint defense of human dignity, peace and well-being. Little good will come of impatience; none at all from apathy.

And this brings me to my final point. What about us non-Romans in the aftermath of Vatican II? The first part of my answer to this question is that, in a curious way, the council has given *us* a charter for change, too. For the blunt truth is that, with Vatican II, the Roman Catholic Church has leapfrogged the rest of us on at least two fronts: church renewal and ecumenical action. And it must also be said that, thus far, non-Roman reaction has been somewhat more negative than the Romans might have had a right to expect. The stance of the World Council of Churches has varied from wary to mulish. Among the Orthodox Churches, only the Ecumenical Patriarchate has been warmly affirmative (and this amounts to less than it might because of the tragically precarious situation of Patriarch Athenagoras, one of the grandest Christians of modern times). Among the non-Roman Churches in the West, only the Anglicans have moved to make much positive out of the new situation. The Methodists did reasonably well *at the council* but at the top levels of church administration we've muffed at least three significant "chances" in the last four years.

But there is finally no evading the challenge of Vatican II that we go and do likewise—with our equivalents of renewal and reform. As far as such words go, this is all old hat to us. But now the Romans have gone and got going with their adventure in reform and renewal while we are still busy with our verbal isometrics (where you stretch your muscles but don't move outside the room). Many of *our* "reformers" are actually malcontents, handier at dismantling existing institutions than replacing them with anything better than modern equivalents of the ancient mystery cults. On the other side, *our* immobilists are at least as intransigent as their Roman counterparts and, what is worse, they are in firm and determined control of our ecclesiastical organizations. Given these upper and nether millstones, it is small wonder that we have a crisis of morale in the Protestant ministry.

Moreover, at a time when constructive theology is having an exciting revival among the Romans, Protestantism is in the throes—temporary, I think—of an acute theological colic, and this is scarcely edifying to our Roman brethren newly interested in Protestant thought. If, for example, you lay Henry deLubac's book on atheism beside the essays of our self-appointed morticians to the Almighty, you might be, as I am, embarrassed for "our side." But the mindless outcry of some of their critics is not very promising, either. If pitiless self-criticism and vigorous bickering between the drivers and the driven were any real aid toward renewal and reform, contemporary Protestantism would surely be on the verge. But something more is required of us—and this is what the Romans did at least in part at Vatican II: the re-opening of the springs and sources of faith itself (the vital sense of the reality and presence of God in our lives, our history and our destiny) the God and Father of our Lord Jesus Christ whose judgments and grace and imperatives are the first and final ground of our existence. Failing a renewal of authentic evangelical religion, we may be nearer the end of the Protestant era than we have thought—but by default and not transfiguration.

Vatican II poses still another challenge to us with respect to our traditional negativism toward Rome. Our forefathers took their stand as "Protestants" before an unreformed and irreformable Roman Catholic Church—and for four centuries we have been justified in that stand by Roman immobilism and triumphalism. After the wars of Religion, this developed into a cozy arrangement in predominantly Protestant countries: the Romans in their ghetto and the Protestants confident that they were the sole trustees of what Paul Tillich too blithely identified as "*the* Protestant principle"—the primacy of faith, the authority of Scripture, the purgation of all idols. Let's skip, just for now, the awkward question as to how "Protestant" Protestants have been, judged by their own chief principle. But we must not fail to notice that Vatican II has taken the Roman Catholic Church a giant step toward the recovery of this very same evangelical tendency, *in a catholic context.* It is, therefore, worth pondering where we would, and should, be if Rome goes on developing the motifs in what is now called her "new theology"—*the primacy of faith, the authority of Scripture, the purgation of all idols:*

What then would happen to our anti-Roman defense mechanisms and our rationalizations of them? It is just as well that our time tonight is gone and that we have to leave this an open question. For it is open—wide-open—and it will not be disposed of by wishful thinking on either side.

Three years ago—when the issue was in honest doubt—I did a little piece that looks more knowledgeable now than it did then—"What if Vatican II *Succeeds?*" [2] My answer then was three-fold: the noses of the immobilists on both sides would be put out of joint; the Romans would find themselves in a fine confusion of transition and change (for which they are ill-prepared); non-Roman Christians would find themselves confronted with the hard choice of shaping up or falling behind. And so it has turned out!

Vatican II *has* succeeded, beyond the hopes of the small cadre of optimists in the beginning. So now we have a similar question that needs asking: What if the Romans *continue to succeed,* even partially, in translating their charters for change into effective, practical programs? For the comfort of the intransigent, it is not at all certain that they will, or even that they can. The bishops are gone from Rome—and so are the observers. The hard-core diehards are still there, dug into their curial foxholes. They are powerful, shrewd and dauntless; they'll never give up or go quietly. Meanwhile, back at the ranch, there's a veritable rash of what looks to old-timers like mutiny in the ranks—Berrigan and Vizzard from the left, Father De Pauw and *The Wanderer* from the right—all volleying and thundering. It should surprise no one that many a bishop is wondering what to do with this Pandora's box they have pried open.

We cannot, then, be certain that the aftermath of Vatican II will match the event itself. What *is* certain is that something momentous is stirring in the Roman Catholic

[2] See above, pp. 62-68.

Church, that there is a vast company of Catholics—intellectuals, professional people, bishops, priests and layfolk —for whom Vatican II was a new lease on life and who have a huge stake in its successful implementation. Between them, they have tremendous resources of talent and dedication; their morale is high; their day, they think, is dawning.

It is, obviously, too soon to cast up anything like a *final* account of Vatican II. We must go on watching this strange upwelling of the tides of the Spirit in the Roman Catholic Church—and not just as passive spectators. We, too, have a stake in their successes. None of us will gain by any failure of theirs. It is, instead, for us to join with them in all the good causes we can, to keep the pressure on all the barriers that are still up and to get on with our own tasks in God's vineyard, but not now in hostile rivalry. Most of all, we must ourselves be ready for the challenges and the frustrations that come with every bid for a better day— ever mindful that Vatican II has planted and we may help water, but it is to the one living God that we *both* look for the increase.

DATE DUE		
MAY 6 '67	DEC 05 1994	
OCT 9 '67	JAN 2 2 1999	
OCT 30 '67 NOV 20 '67	SEP 1 3 2000	
MAY 13 '68 NOV 24		
	JAN 0 6 2005	
APR 16 '70	FEB 0 8 2008	
DEC 17 '72		
MAR 28 '73		
	AUG 17 2020	
AUG 18 '74		
DEC 12 '74		
FEB 17 '75		
MAR 15 '77		
APR 5 '78		
AUG 18 1983		
OCT 27 1994		
NOV 21 1994		
GAYLORD		PRINTED IN U.S.A